LEARNING
to WALK in
INDIA

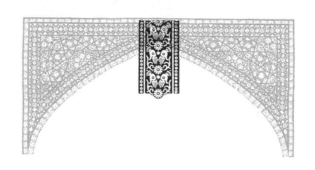

LEARNING
to WALK in
INDIA

a love story

MOLLY KATE BROWN

diamond sky press
BOULDER, COLORADO USA

Published by Diamond Sky Press
ISBN 978-0-9966166-0-7
Chapter 7, the angel card excerpt is from Saints & Angels Oracle Cards by Doreen Virtue (Hay House, 2005).

This book is dedicated to all beings,
seen and unseen. And to the vast ocean from which we arise,
little wave expressions of the all-that-is-or-ever-will-be,
the eternal divine.

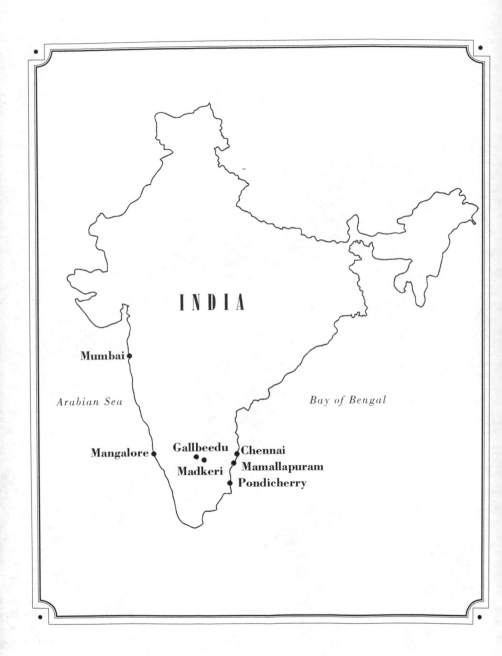

part one

The single most sacred pilgrimage
you will ever make is the one
right where you are.

1

I'm drowning. In this sea of sixteen million people I'm searching for a stronghold, sure footing, some security to ease my escalating desperation. I face Mumbai, teeming with humanity in its various masquerades—the young, the old, the starving, the rich, the destitute—alone. I'm a thirty-two-year-old white American woman facing India by myself. This is what I wanted. What I asked for. I've always been partial to the head-first Aries approach into the deep end, but this body of water has a rip-roaring current. While I do know how to swim, I am not sure I'm equipped to swim in these waters. Last night when I watched my beloved husband Dan leave for the airport in Chennai on his way back to our home in Colorado—our one-month honeymoon in southern India had come to an end, and I was off on my solo Indian journey as long planned—there was a little voice in my heart that said *go with him*.

Grimacing, I take a deep breath and make my way through Chatrapati Shivaji International Airport. Outside I am met by an onslaught—touts, the most excruciatingly persistent sellers of everything; homeless people; clamoring cab drivers; scantily clad dirty children who are well versed in the fingers-to-mouth gesture, the universal sign of hunger—and the level of noise that accompanies this scene for me, both inwardly and outwardly, is shocking. I feel like I'm submerged neck-deep in an airtight container with a rapidly rising water level. You see, something is wrong with my knees. My very support in this physical world is faltering. Initially I thought they were sore from being cramped on the overnight train that Dan and I took from the southwest Indian state of Karnataka to Chennai on the east coast two nights before. But they've been growing in size and are becoming ever more painful by the second.

There is a knowing from some very deep, quiet place inside that something is askew. My adrenaline is on the rise, queuing up a state of panic as beads of sweat drip from my forehead and my armpits grow damp.

Entropy is a universal phenomenon, a law of nature whereby disorder in a system increases. A less-probable more-ordered state gives way to a more-probable less-ordered state. Things tend toward the random, toward chaos. Perfect internal disorder, they say, a form of equilibrium. Things dissolve—mountains, seas, species, planets, galaxies, universes, relationships, personalities, the dinosaurs, the human race—on their way to less order and more chaos, and give way to what?

That is what I'm feeling—disorder with a side of panic, the rising water threatening to extinguish my breath, to annihilate me. Panic lurks like the grim reaper in the shadows between the parked cabs, shifting dastardly between the cramped hot spaces, hiding behind the people spread out before me. When I took physics some years back, something in me was fascinated and drawn to that universal phenomenon of entropy. But at that time I wasn't unraveling in India. Now I feel the strings of my safety net being snipped one at a time. Ping. Ping. Ping. I'm slipping and clinging desperately to something rather unstable that is quickly disappearing before me. I sense a massive void, and it is terrifying.

As I prepare to leave the safety of the airport, I can still hear the tourist official's parting words of advice: "Take a metered cab." At once I am singled out by an immensely persuasive Indian man clad in a once-off-white short-sleeve shirt tucked into a snug, wraparound *lungi*, wide brown feet bare on the warm Mumbai asphalt.

"Come, come," he insists, pulling me along with his persistent hand gestures in a palpable air of authority. His neck thrusts out like a chicken's in unison with his emphatic hand gesticulations, propelling his chin forward and causing his eyes to grow so large they look as though they might pop right out of their sockets. At least three inches shorter than me, the little man assures me he will get me where I need to go. As if he or I have any idea where that is.

"Can you take me to a bus station?" I ask.

"Yes, yes," he replies, accompanied by a head wagging back and forth from left to right in the quintessential Indian head bob that can mean either "Yes," "I hear you," "I understand," "I acknowledge," or any amalgamation thereof. To the untrained eye it would appear that the head bob is a "no" or an "I don't know," but his is accompanied by an emphatic "yes" and I believe him. When you are unraveling and your adrenaline level is surging, it's easy to be confused.

The tourist official's words reverberate inside of me as we approach what turns out to be an auto rickshaw, not a cab. This is a red flag, but the little Indian man's persuasiveness coupled with my desire to walk as little as possible due to the stabbing pain in both of my knees, lands me at his mercy inside of the auto rickshaw, an open-air two-to-three (or ten) seater that resembles an Indian version of the golf cart, only it can be filled way beyond capacity and has a raucous horn. We pull out into the throng of moving vehicles—cabs, cars, trucks, buses—their horns blaring as they vie for the lead. Overstimulation sets in and I lose the ability to hear myself think.

Barely a moment or two later, he hits the brake and pulls over to the curb.

"Why are you pulling over?" I demand.

An impertinent hand waves in my face. There is no bus station in sight. The man climbs out and approaches the cab parked in front of us next to the curb. He starts chatting up the driver, cordially leaning into the cab, arms folded and resting on the open window. No doubt they're in cahoots. He gestures emphatically for me to climb into the cab, his hand pointing into its shady interior. I grab my backpack and climb out of the rickshaw, waving my finger back and forth at him, spewing something about truth and shame and his mother as if he understands or cares. Meanwhile my mind is spinning with the legend of the weary traveler who wakes up in a hotel bathtub missing a kidney, which is by then being sold on the black market somewhere in southeast Asia.

I raise my hand into the air to hail my own cab. The air is thick, hot, and effused with the scent of smoke and urine. A fly lands on my face, scurries over my lips, though I repeatedly swat it away. I make eye contact with the penetrating, dark brown eyes of a driver as he approaches. Feeling a sense of relief, I climb into his cab. He is a rather large Muslim man with a long black unkempt beard. He is such a large man that he barely fits in the driver's seat. His turban and flowing white clothing are stained with the sweat of Mumbai. His skin shines with it in the late morning heat. Tufts of hair poke out from his ears and climb out of his tunic at his neck.

"I will get you to a bus station," he assures me in a calm, brotherly manner. I believe him. Turns out the bus station is a wooden bench on the side of a very busy road.

"Cheap gov'mnt bus," he explains. It is very kind that he is trying to help me out by saving me a few rupees. I don't have the strength or courage to tell him that I don't want a cheap government bus—that I am an American woman in dire need of air-conditioning, soft seats, and some semblance of security.

Being left alone to fend for myself among the masses on a bench on the side of a busy road in Mumbai is simply too much to bear. But since I don't have the courage to tell him this due to some early construct that has me desperately not wanting to offend anyone for fear of the ensuing discomfort that might arise in me if I do, I find myself alone on a bench on the side of a dusty, traffic-laden road in Mumbai. Panic is no longer lurking in the shadows. It is now center stage—dancing in front of me as adrenaline course through my veins. Meanwhile, my knees still don't want to do what knees are supposed to do and they now look like someone else's knees—hot, red, swollen beyond recognition—not like my sexy thirty-two-year-old-yoga-doin'-running knees. It feels like someone is pressing on them with the flat metal head of a large hammer. It keeps pressing even though I'm screaming *MERCY!* My ability to walk is diminishing by the hour. I push further to the periphery the helpless feeling of desperation pulsing through every cell of my body. I cling to the notion that if I can make it to the meditation center several hours northeast of Mumbai in Igatpuri where I am scheduled for a meditation retreat in a couple of days, everything will be fine.

Eventually a bus pulls up, its breaks squealing as the smell of exhaust fills my nose. The destination is written in Hindi on the front above the windshield. I don't speak or read Hindi. I climb the steps with the difficulty of a ninety-year-old woman, trying to appear as though I am in no discomfort whatsoever, fighting tears as intense pain stabs my knees again and again.

"Is this bus going to Igatpuri?" I ask, my voice quivering.

In very limited English the bus driver explains it goes *by* Igatpuri on its way to Nasik and that he will drop me off on the road outside of Igatpuri. At least I think that is what he is saying. My heart sinks. I take up the seat behind the driver, having been informed by seasoned travelers that that's where a female traveling alone in India should sit to avoid being harassed by less-than-scrupulous men. I squirm and fidget, stretching both legs out toward the aisle, then one leg up on the seat.

"Dropped off on the side of the road?" I confirm. Half head bob in response. He collects my bus fare, taking five times what he takes from the Indian passengers, but I am too worn down to argue. I imagine myself dropped off in the middle of Nowhere, India, hardly able to walk.

The bus begins its slow journey through the massive city.

Through the metal bars of the open windows I feel the heat blazing off of the concrete and smell its scent. The air is thick with auto fumes, the smoke of fires, myriad gastronomic scents from tandooris and stove tops. I smell overpowering odors of bodies and the pungent smells of garlic and other spices that cling to them as they file past me on the bus at various stops in the city. The whole scene— Mumbai, her scent, the passage of the outside world through the bus window with the blazing sun in the sky—is dizzying, and it presses down on me with the weight of its heat. The bus finally crawls into a bus station on our way out of Mumbai. From somewhere in my depths I register a flickering bulletin: ABORT MISSION, it reads, flashing in bright neon orange with that soft electric sound made by flashing neon signs in B-rated movies that take place at deserted hotels in the desert Southwest. Better to be in Mumbai in this state, some rational part of me decides, than dropped off on the side of a road in a village three hours away. When the bus comes to a stop at the bus station, I grab my backpack and hobble down the steps onto the safety of the Mumbai concrete.

Walking slowly and gingerly I approach a little stand in the humid, open-air bus station. I buy a Coke and a pack of Gold Flake cigarettes. I haven't smoked in ages, but this situation is providing the perfect excuse to indulge. I smoked my way through my twenties, always the most when I traveled, and during stressful situations. The present situation is meeting all of the aforementioned so I limp on over to an unoccupied concrete bench in the center of all of it, light up, and inhale deeply. I scan the bus station as I exhale, becoming painfully aware that I am *the* object of attention. I've always been averse to being the center of attention. It makes my skin prickly and makes me sweat. Here in India it is anxiety inducing. I thought the *salwar kameez* I was wearing—a long tunic overlaying loose trouser-like pants—would camouflage me, like a lizard on a rock that assumes he can't be seen if he stays perfectly still, that he'll just blend right in. I'm a white woman dressed in a *salwar kameez*, alone, gimpy, anxiety-stricken, and chain-smoking in this tiny little bus station. If I were them, I'd be staring at me curiously, too.

Sinking into the bench, I open my Lonely Planet and flip through the section on Mumbai, desperately seeking a plan. Something in me still equates a plan with security. Let's get on with blowing that notion to bits.

2

Last night as I was saying goodbye to my husband in a clean, safe hotel room in Chennai on the other side of the Indian sub-continent, I had the sense that a lifetime with this man would never be enough. Besides the fact that he is gorgeous and I am madly in love with him, he is the only person I can imagine sitting in bed with predawn, sipping tea in silence as the day awakens from slumber and the sky morphs from soft gray to blue in that profound early morning stillness that isn't found at any other time of the day. In fact, he is the only man I've been with who fixes me that tea, and the second and third cup as well. His strong, soft, humble presence makes the minutia of life seem like no big thing. It continually reminds me that there is nothing to be done other than to return to the very moment before me—that swirling, eddying, dynamic eternal instant that isn't even an instant at all. His presence is deeply unwavering and supportive to the effulgence of my being. What moves between us is truth unadulterated—his and mine meeting in a crucible of sanctity in which we both can unfold. I adore his presence because it reminds me of the truth that I am in the moments that I forget. One look in his dreamy green eyes draws my insides out.

I didn't want to let him go, but it was time to face India on my own. My India journey had been in the making since before I knew Dan. When we fell in love and decided to get married he agreed to come for the first month as a honeymoon, and I would then continue alone for a few months to do whatever it was I needed to do in India.

In the sanctuary where we spent our last few hours together—replete with shiny, white toilet, sparkling clean shower, large bed with fluffy white comforter—my knees were just beginning to give the faintest hint that something was awry. I brushed the discomfort off as a result of being cramped on the overnight train the night before. Our one-month honeymoon was ending, and he was flying home as planned. "I love you, baby," I said as I gazed into his large green eyes. "I love you more," he replied with his usual response. My dear friend Cynthia told me once years ago that you always want to marry a guy who loves you more than you love him. Just because he bends over backwards for me more than I bend over backwards for him, or because he never snaps at me the way I snap at him, doesn't mean he loves me more, does it? Couldn't it just mean that I am more fire with a shorter fuse?

I said goodbye to him in that hotel room, holding him fast and tight. When it was time, he picked up his tiny daypack—all that my minimalist husband brought along—and walked out of the hotel room to make his international flight. Staring through the peephole I stood sentinel by the door, desperately longing to see his handsome face return for one last kiss. I waited and waited. I failed to anticipate how difficult it would be to say goodbye to him.

I wasn't seeking anything by traveling to India—I was simply drawn to her. She began to pull at my umbilical region, hooking her talons into the visceral layers of my core. The desire to travel to her and experience god-only-knows-what began to intensify during the two years I spent planning the India journey, and then I set out like so many other travelers before me, succumbing to the pull like a moth surrendering to the flame. Unknowingly, I was setting out to have my patience, compassion, understanding, tolerance, faith— my very being—tested in ways I never imagined. I did not realize it at the time, but I was traveling to India as a move toward having my myths about myself shattered—undone from their roots—a move toward disorder to achieve equilibrium. Of course when I was planning the trip, all I knew was that I needed to get there. I needed to experience her. I didn't know why.

I'd been practicing Vipassana meditation for some years. The word *vipassana* means to see things as they really are. Vipassana meditation is a powerful tool for disarming the mind. In fact, one of the sharpest tools I've ever encountered. The main center, Dhamma Giri—one of many Vipassana centers around the world—is in Igatpuri, which is three hours northeast of Mumbai by bus or train. That's where I was headed when forced to abort mission.

I'd had my own version of a spiritual practice since I was in my teens. It wasn't a formal practice—it was just what my heart was called to do. I'd light a candle in my bedroom at night and sit quietly in the silence with the flickering light, speaking to the universe, the divine—giving my thanks, saying my prayers, asking to be a servant. I would keep sitting, and giving my thanks, and keep conversing with the all-that-is as I was inspired to do.

I explored a formal meditation practice in Boulder, Colorado, where I'd moved from Virginia when I was twenty-three. It didn't really stick. When I was twenty-eight I was on a road trip in Utah with my then passionate, wild Australian fiancé. We stopped overnight in Moab to stay with a friend of his. His friend's wife told me about her meditation practice called Vipassana. She said it was taught at ten-day silent meditation retreats, and there was no charge for the retreats. The courses were run on donations from students. Something about that spoke to the purity of this specific tradition for me. I was very drawn to the idea of ten days of silence like that moth to the flame. Immediately I knew I would go sit, and I knew I would do it soon. Something in me craved it. Michelle, the friend's wife (later to become my dear friend), held a signpost for me that day.

By the time I got to India I'd been sitting ten-day courses regularly for some years. I reasoned that a ten-day course would be the best way to begin the solo part of my journey in India. Meditating in silence for a period of time can result in profound wisdom and clarity, as the white lotus flower arises from the depths of the murky water in which it takes root. For me this has been a very intelligent way to deal with self-made structures, as well as fear and its tendrils of contraction that arise from my conditioning. It helps me move from a place of thrashing about in the water to a place of treading—calmly, clearly. It's not that the experience all of a sudden becomes totally pleasant, or even that I am seeking what feels pleasant. But there eventually comes an allowing of everything that shows up, and thus the struggle falls away. There is even an allowing of the struggle if it is there.

The visual analogy that arises is a deep sea with a bed of kelp anchored in at the ocean floor. At the depth, the kelp moves about with the current but the movement is minimal, gentle. The currents are surely there, but the movement of the kelp is subtler, as the currents are not as strong closer to the ocean floor where the kelp is rooted in. Toward the surface farther away from its roots, the kelp thrashes about more. Things are more turbulent and the currents much stronger at the surface. If we forget that we are actually rooted down at the depth, rooted right into the Source, we become the kelp at the surface, reacting and thrashing. If we remember that we are actually anchored into something much deeper, our being-ness can arise from this place, and life is oh-so-much smoother. This is what Vipassana has been for me—a constant remembering, a life raft back to the Truth, back to the Source, every time. Something inside of me reasoned that I'd need this once Dan left and I was on my own in India.

After I said goodbye to Dan, I spent a fairly sleepless night in the hotel room, awake with the anxiety that comes from being alone in a totally foreign place with the not-yet-conscious knowledge that something big was brewing inside of me. With some trepidation I arose at four o'clock in the morning to test the knees. They were huge, red, and stiff. I was having difficulty walking. I paced the room, back and forth, back and forth, trying to walk the stiffness out of them. They seemed to loosen up a little. I took a steaming hot shower and gathered my belongings. I put on my teal paisley *salwar kameez*, wrapping the matching scarf around my neck so that it draped down my back, coming to rest on the thigh-length tunic that hung loosely from my shoulders. My loose cotton pants were made from the same fabric. I had two of these outfits made when Dan and I were traveling together. I paused, looking at myself in the full-length mirror.

We were in Mamallapuram then, only several days into our honeymoon. Dan waited patiently as I sifted through piles of brightly colored, ornately printed fabric while the male shopkeepers looked on. Finally I came to the teal color, with its black paisley pattern. I held it up for Dan to see. He nodded, leaning patiently against the entrance to the fabric shop, the breeze tousling his thick, black curls that were succumbing to the humidity. In less than three minutes, the dark-skinned southern Indian men had taken my measurements and my money. Two days later I had two new outfits—a teal one and some version of a deep fuchsia. They helped me feel a little less conspicuous as we wandered our way through southern India.

Dan swore up and down that he was *not* going to wear any Indian clothing. His olive-green Smartwool travel T-shirt would work just fine. Whoever invented that travel shirt had clearly not been to southern India. Before we left Mamallapuram, Dan was wearing a loose, white linen tunic and even lighter pants. His *sammy kameez*, he called it.

I tried to convince myself that everything was going to be fine as I gazed in the mirror. *I'm a grown woman, for god's sake. I know plenty of people who have traveled in India alone.* I burst into tears.

17

The tears did wonders for the pink hue that remained cast against the whites of my eyes since I'd developed a bilateral pussy eye infection the week before. The thirty-two-year-old woman staring back at me, clad in her deep teal *salwar kameez*, looked far more together than *I* felt. She didn't appear to be unraveling.

I picked up the phone in the hotel room to call my friend Laurie, who happens to be a nurse practitioner. I knew if anyone could help me, it would be her. Laurie has traveled extensively throughout India and Asia, volunteering along the way in underserved communities and refugee camps. She is a wealth of information when it comes to health in the developing world. I knew that she would have some idea what was going on with my knees and eyes. It would be New Year's Eve back in Boulder. I prayed that she would answer.

The year before my India travels began, two people from completely different areas of my life who knew of my India plans told me I needed to meet Laurie as she also lived in Boulder and had volunteered in India fairly extensively. They knew I too was intending to volunteer there. One of them sent me her contact information via e-mail. I had every intention of getting in touch with her eventually, but I was planning Dan's and my wedding and organizing a meditation course, so I had not yet found the time to do so.

Seven months before my travels began, I was sitting at the registration table for a Vipassana meditation course. It was a beautiful spring day, and a deep-blue Colorado sky framed the ponderosa pines that filled the air with their vanilla scent. The sunshine was filtered into dancing dappled light. Ravens squawked overhead. A woman with sparkly-blue eyes approached me and handed me her completed application. I looked at the name on the form.

"Are you Laurie Lee, the nurse practitioner in *Boulder*?" I asked.

"I am," she replied, smiling at me.

"I've been told by two people from completely different areas of my life to contact you. My friend's mom actually sent me your phone number. It's in my inbox. I've been meaning to call you."

"Well, here I am," she said, not at all surprised. "In fact, I am not really supposed to be here," she went on to explain. "I was supposed to be volunteering in East Timor, but because of civil unrest and a broken bone in my hand, I decided it would be better not to go now. Anyway, I was due for a ten-day," she said, referring to the meditation course.

Thus began a fast friendship. After our ten days of silence were over and we were able to speak, our affinity for one another became apparent. I dialed the number and it began to ring. One ring. Two rings. *Please* answer. Three rings.

"Hello," a warm and familiar voice said on the other end.

"Laurie, it's Molly," I managed, through upheavals of sobs that erupted once I heard her voice.

"Molly *Brown?*" she asked with surprise.

"Yes," I began. "Laurie, something is wrong with me. I have no idea what's going on. My knees started hurting yesterday, and now it's difficult to walk. Dan is gone, and I am pretty much freaking out."

She didn't tell me she was in the middle of serving dinner at her New Year's Eve party. Rather, she patiently listened to my entire story, and with her enormous heart she reassured me. She surmised it was one of two things—either a tendonitis caused by the antibiotic I was taking for a bout of dysentery that had returned a few days earlier (the second time in my four weeks in India) or a reactive arthritis as a result of the dysentery.

"You'll be fine. Just get to the meditation course and you'll be fine. I've never had any trouble with the food making me sick at the meditation courses in India," she assured me. We were both aware that the nature of these meditation courses is such that physical ailments sometimes disappear. I was banking on this.

I felt uplifted and confident that I should continue on to Mumbai. I left the hotel in the dark in a rickshaw on my way to the airport. There was no one around at that hour. The streets of Chennai were quiet. My rickshaw driver didn't say much as we rode in the silent stillness just before dawn.

I looked around and thought to myself, *I can handle this.*

I became aware that the rickshaw was slowing down and making its way to the side of the road. My adrenaline level surged until I realized our vector. There on the side of the road was a small makeshift Ganesh temple. The driver steered the rickshaw until we came to idle in front of it. He bowed his hands in prayer in front of his face, eyes closed, and stayed that way for a moment, lips moving silently, carrying the contents of his heart out into the open air, into the eternal web of life. Candles and incense burned in the darkness, and my heart was relieved, renewed. When he was finished, he said nothing but shifted the idling rickshaw into gear and drove off into the soft, warm morning. *Thank you,* I uttered silently. *Thank you.*

With the exception of a young Indian man who gave me obscene tongue gestures every time our eyes met—like he was thoroughly enjoying a melting ice-cream cone—the plane ride to Mumbai was uneventful. Instead of being appalled or afraid of him, I was simply annoyed, as I would be at a persistent, buzzing mosquito. I did my best not to look at him and to observe the physical sensation of irritation arising inside of me.

I'd taken Imodium to keep the diarrhea at bay for my day of travel. Once the plane touched down in India's largest city, I darted into its tiny bathroom. All morning I'd been spared, but just as the plane landed, the urge overcame me. I spent at least ten minutes in the bowels of that plane dealing with my bowels. When I felt it was safe I tried to exit and the lavatory door was forced closed by passengers eager to disembark. They exited from the rear of the plane, and when I was finally able to open the door, I was the only remaining passenger.

A long, steep staircase taunted me like a dare from the school-yard bully. Inhaling deeply I began to navigate the stairs slowly, one at a time, to the bus that was headed to the terminal. I was aware that all of the other passengers were watching me. I squeezed my way onto the bus—standing room only—and realized I was in di-rect view of Obscene Tongue Man. He did indeed show me the in-side of his mouth again, and it took immense restraint not to show him my middle finger. Not that he would know what it meant. With my luck, it would probably mean come-home-with-me-tonight.

I was able to locate the tourist desk within the airport just as the diarrhea assaulted me again. I scurried to the nearest bathroom only to discover that it was a hole in the floor. I certainly couldn't squat because of the pain in my knees, so I gave it my best aim, trying to keep my clean *salwar kameez* out of the impact. I didn't know whether to laugh or cry. An hour later I was in a little bus station in Mumbai, chain-smoking Gold Flakes and in desperate need of a plan.

3

I'm pleased as punch to have an excuse to smoke. I quit because I'd seen firsthand as a cardiac nurse what it does to people. The site of an elderly person with an ashen-gray face from years of smoking, pillows propped several deep behind the back in an attempt to be as upright as possible in order to catch the breath, and anxiety in the eyes due to a lack of oxygen from severely damaged lungs, is not a pretty sight. Smoking is a lethal habit and I know that. Now that I have a husband who I adore, I want to maximize my time on the planet with him. Besides, it smells wretched, turns my fingers yellow, and makes my chest feel tight in a painful kind of way. But that doesn't change the fact that I find something immensely pleasurable about the act of it, and this state I'm in—lack of control, uncertainty, unknown, and adrenaline on the rise—is *such* an excuse to go for it.

I flip through my guidebook until I read about an area of Mumbai called Colaba. It's purported to be so full of tourists that a Westerner hardly stands out. In my condition I have no desire to stand out at all. After my warmish Coke and too many cigarettes, I summon the courage to rise and face Mumbai again. I reason that after a night's rest in Mumbai I will feel better and be able to travel on to Igatpuri. Never mind that my swollen knees have begun to resemble ruby red grapefruits and walking is so excruciatingly painful that it takes my breath away.

After an insufferably hot cab ride past the Victoria Terminus—India's busiest train station—into lively, clamoring Colaba with its throng of Indians and Westerners flowing like a river down each side of the road, eddies swirling about endless vendors selling wares and goods, colors streaming forth in the form of saris and silks, I arrive in an overpriced hotel room. Christmas season in Mumbai is one of the most popular times for weddings and tourists. The bargains that apply in most of India do not apply here now. My accommodation is equipped with a sit-down Western toilet for which I have paid a pretty rupee, as squatting is no longer an option. It also has a fairly decent tiled shower. I throw my backpack on the bed and head into the small bathroom, throwing open the window to light up. I sit on the toilet seat, watching the smoke swirling and curling its way out of the screen through tiny holes. I desperately need that plan.

I also need to recharge my international calling card, so I leave the safety of the hotel in the late afternoon, determined to make it to the nearest Internet café several blocks away. As soon as my feet hit the concrete I'm approached rather brazenly by a dirt-stained, sylph-like, anorexic-looking Indian girl who cannot be more than eighteen years old. I can see through visible layers of filth to her raw beauty—her big dark eyes, full lips, long wavy hair, smooth skin, her delicate frame. I smell alcohol on her breath.

"Whatever you want, I get it for you," she says.

I keep walking and she follows me, determined to be of service.

"I get you anything," she says, in a soft, quivering voice.

I turn around and look her firmly in the eye.

"I'm sick and I don't have time for this," I say, trying to give the appearance of one who is not in immense amounts of pain, doing my best not to limp. I continue walking, staring straight ahead. She disappears back into the shadows. I press on, not looking anyone in the eyes. I'm in no mood to engage. My knees are eliciting the kind of pain about to have its way with you, the kind that drives you off of your feet and into a fetal position as your breath becomes shallow. It's lucky that my hotel is off the main drag and that the several back-street blocks to the Internet café aren't too crowded. Awash with dark humor when I finally find the café and realize I have to climb a steep, spiral staircase to reach the computers, I can't help but be totally amused.

The part of me that consciously chooses the inner journey as *the* priority in my life and experiences this life as a classroom wants to view the impasse as an opportunity. The fearful child in me who is approaching helpless and desperately wants her mamma is about to burst into tears. I climb the stairs slowly, one by one. I'm sweating, nauseated with the pain. I drag myself up each step using the railing as a crutch. When I reach the computer room at the top, I'm somewhat relieved to find myself surrounded by Westerners. I am in too much distress to reach out to anyone, but it is reassuring nonetheless. I log onto the website for my phone card and attempt to recharge it.

"Denial ain't just a river in Egypt," Mark Twain apparently said. Evening is descending as I walk slowly back to the hotel, so slowly and deliberately that I appear to be avoiding cracking eggshells beneath me. I am acutely aware that the rate of acceleration of my knee deterioration situation could equate to my being unable to walk at all in the ensuing hours. It is dawning on me that I need medical attention. I need a hospital.

Once back in the safety of my room, I attempt to use my calling card to call home but the polite computerized woman's voice tells me there are no minutes left on my card. Evidently, my attempt to recharge the card was not successful. I burst into sobs—hysterical, gut-wrenching sobs. The bed shakes as I sob right out of me the fear and anguish I have been contending with all day. And then just for kicks I begin sorting through some of the fears I've been contending with my entire life. It feels like an appropriate time to dump some crap that I've been stuffing—to get it all out there—so I let the tears flow unimpeded.

For starters, there is fear of the unknown. This includes (but is not limited to) the uncertainty of what the future holds. Not just the immediate future, but the future in the big-picture sense. Boy, does that one cause tension in my body with the need to control things, to hold it all together, to "have a plan." To appear to myself that I know what the hell I'm doing.

There is a disparity between how I experience success and how I was conditioned to experience it. Success to me is resting in the absolute stillness and certainty of eternal being and experiencing *that*. It is feeling a breeze gently tickling my cheek. Witnessing dancing dapples of sunlight on a shaded forest floor. Smelling the dank, rich earth on a warm summer evening. Hearing drops of rain hit the roof or watching them fall from the sky. Listening to the wind dance through the tops of the pine trees or flutter the aspen leaves. Or waves continually lapping onto the shore and then receding back into the ocean, again and again. Bearing witness to spring blossoms worn on a fruit tree like her finest ball gown—and how her branches reach into the sky in a brilliant form of expression, like she's striking a pose for her beloved Eternal. A brilliant dew-kissed cobweb shimmering with diamonds and quivering in the morning light. Pure, intimate connection with another human being. That degree of simplicity makes my heart sing. It stops my breath and moves my being to tears. And that's success to me. The world from which I emerged views success differently—stated or not—and the internal structures I created from an early age as a result of that creates tension in me.

Fear of abandonment. That one was imprinted on my little soul when my dad left. I was eighteen months old. It was preconceptual so I have no visual memory of him leaving. But I have finally accessed the feelings of grief that my little being experienced as a result. And to protect myself, my little ego created ways of being that assisted me in not ever feeling that horribleness again. I learned to please others at the expense of myself. I learned not to speak my heart, my truth, for fear of rocking the boat and offending anyone (and ultimately not wanting to experience that discomfort)—even a hairy cab driver wanting to drop me off on a bench on the side of the road in Mumbai. I began asking *what's wrong with me?* at a very early age, because to my little soul something was wrong with me if my dad left—and my inner critic has been having a field day with that one ever since. It led to my needing others' approval or validation of what or who I am. And while those structures are crumbling (thank God), they aren't gone completely. I know this because if they had totally dissolved, I could hear another's slanderous words of me and have absolutely zero internal reaction to it. While I no longer need to react verbally to that person, internal reaction still arises.

When my dad left, my mom had to survive and raise three kids, me being the middle child. I quickly learned to be okay because my brother was a baby at six months, and my sister eighteen months my senior needed my mom more than I did. If I was okay it meant I'd be loved and not abandoned again. I took on the role of being okay (stuffing my real feelings of sadness, anger, grief—anything other than the okay) and my true young self stopped being herself in order to be okay. I shape shifted and therefore my true little self wasn't seen. Not in the Na'vi way of being seen in the movie *Avatar*. The *I see you* way that they see each other. Those early ways of being solidified and turned into behaviors in the world to avoid the fear and terror my little heart felt when I was eighteen months old. I am sure those ways of being—that ultimately are ways of not being myself—are the source of wicked migraine headaches I've had since childhood. So there is a broken-hearted, grieving eighteen-month-old who is finally shedding her tears, too. She is just fine with India letting her bleeding, raw heart have a turn.

India feels like a ripe place to shed these tears—to let those tensions and constructs unravel in a pile of messiness. The sobs shake me like I've never been shaken before. Then there is fear of death, of annihilation—a big one. That one lurks just underneath the fear of abandonment, slightly out of reach of my consciousness. I haven't fully gotten into it yet but I am aware it is there. The next big root to be unearthed. How do I come to terms with the knowledge that I will dissolve back into the emptiness from which I came? Annihilated in that entropic way. There is no control there. No planning to be done. And I'll be going at it alone—at least in the by myself sense. Won't be taking my family and friends on that ride. There's fear there for sure. *Oh God, what if that annihilation comes tonight?*

I let the sobs work me as you might knead a ball of dough thoroughly until there are no more lumps and bumps to be worked out. Through some minor miracle, I somehow find my breath and stay with it. When the sobs abate I light a Gold Flake cigarette. Through puffy, bloodshot eyes I watch the smoke swirl into little plumes before they disappear into naught. I'd like to disappear into naught.

I gather my few unpacked items. One thing is for sure, if I am going to an Indian hospital I am going to do so clean because I don't know how long it will be before I take another shower. I make my way into the bathroom and carefully lower myself to the shower floor. The cool tile beneath me is soothing to my naked body. I hug myself. I rock back and forth under the warm water, a stranger's legs stretched out before me with their intensely swollen knees, missing my husband so fiercely that my chest aches. I tell myself repeatedly that I'm okay. I wash my hair, scrubbing and massaging my scalp, letting the warm water run over me for what feels like a very long time. I examine my knees, wondering what in God's name is going on with them. When I'm sufficiently clean, I hoist myself to a standing position using the windowsill.

I dress in clean clothes and pull out my guidebook to see what it says about area hospitals. According to the Lonely Planet, Breach Candy Hospital is the best hospital in Mumbai, if not India. I call downstairs to let the hotel know I need a cab to go to the hospital.

The doorman arrives within minutes to help me with my bag. I hand him the remainder of the cigarettes. He accepts them with half a head bob and a warm smile. Downstairs at the desk I ask for a refund. I'm denied with another polite bob of the head.

A cab is waiting when I reach the entrance to the hotel. I ask the doorman to be sure the driver understands that I want to go to Breach Candy Hospital. After the events of the day I have little capacity for any diversion in my plan. With a last glance around, I back into the backseat of the cab, butt first. I stretch my legs out on the seat. As we are pulling away from the curb, I catch a glimpse of the young Indian girl watching me from the shadows. Her fear and mine meet in a place devoid of words.

We drive north from Colaba, following the lights that glitter on the blackness of the Arabian Sea, which appears to move like a giant serpent in a slow motion sway, spine curving out left then right then left again. To my surprise I feel rather calm watching young couples stroll on the sidewalk by the sea. I begin to feel—in the big picture sense—that I am not alone. That knowledge seeps out of somewhere deep in my being. I welcome the sense of calm that ensues.

There is a strong smell of spicy cologne in the cab, and the driver has upbeat Hindi music playing. The night air is warm and humid and its numinous presence filters into the cab from the street and the sea beyond, mussing my hair and kissing my cheek. I am not familiar with the smell of this night.

"Where are you from?" I ask.

"I from Varanasi. Holy city," he says, head wagging and pearly whites peeking from behind a wide grin as he studies me in the rearview mirror.

"Do you ever go back there to visit?"

"Once I go back I have four children now. Oldest in college," he says, as the sweet Indian intonation dances from word to word.

I hear about his four children, his wife, his religion. He is quite happy to lure me into the portal of his existence, and I am even happier to go there. A profound sense of peace pervades me. I feel safe. When at last we pull up to Breach Candy Hospital, I take my bag and thank him for the ride.

"I wait for you," he says, head wagging in declaration.

"I don't think I'll be leaving the hospital tonight."

He thrusts his card at me through the open window. "When you ready to leave hospital, I come," he says. I take his card and thank him and watch as his red taillights pull back out into the Mumbai traffic.

4

Even though it is after dark, there are people milling about at the hospital entrance. I feel their eyes boring into me as I approach the security officer.

"Which way to the emergency room?" I ask. He points to a door a little further down on the outside of the building. By this time, I am walking so cautiously that a crawling baby could outpace me. My heavy backpack is making it all the more awkward. Every step is an excruciating exercise in *The Little Engine That Could—I think I can, I think I can*. A marathon in *what are you made of, sister?*

The emergency door is the finish line and I focus on it with the dogged determination that comes with being born of the first sign of the Zodiac—the fire sign, Aries. As I approach the door, it opens and out walks a handsome, well-dressed man, appearing to be in his late thirties. He is wearing khaki pants and a short-sleeved white shirt. He has short black hair and his eyes are a muted amalgamation of hazel and green.

"What is the problem?" he inquires in beautiful English layered with an Indian accent.

"Who are you?" I ask.

"I am the doctor," he says. I take a deep breath and exhale with relief.

"My knees have become so swollen and painful over the last twenty-four hours that I am having trouble walking. I've had dysentery off and on for the last couple of weeks, and several days ago I developed a bilateral eye infection." Despite ardent protest from my knees, I shift my stance from one leg to the other in a desperate effort to remain standing.

"I went to an ER in Mangalore when I was traveling in the

south. They gave me an antibiotic for the diarrhea and I took it until this morning. I'm still using antibiotic drops in my eyes for the infection, but it is mostly gone."

"Let me look at your knees," he says.

I pull up my pant legs so he can see the swollen ruby red grapefruits.

"This is an emergency, yes?" he asks rhetorically.

"That's why I'm here. I'm almost unable to walk."

"Come," he commands, and I am grateful. I don't want to be in charge anymore. India has exhausted me. He doesn't offer to carry my bag, so I follow him through the ER, heavy awkward backpack slung over my shoulder, to an empty gurney surrounded by a white curtain.

He examines my knees more carefully and listens to my lungs. A nurse smiles at me while she takes my vital signs. They leave me lying alone behind the curtain. I hear him speaking to someone on the phone. His hazel-green eyes peer around the curtain.

"You need to be admitted," he says.

"I know."

"You will need to pay for your stay here," he continues.

"Not a problem, I assure you. I have cash and a credit card." Thank God I had the foresight to exchange some traveler's checks before Dan and I parted company. The doctor leaves me alone again.

After I've been lying there for some time, a second physician by the name of Dr. Jain arrives to see me. Everything about Dr. Jain exudes compassion. His features are soft. I guess him to be in his mid-to-late forties. When he looks at me, he seems to do so curiously, from large deep brown eyes. He, too, is well dressed, and his moves are graceful and gentle. After examining me and listening attentively to my story, from beginning to end, he tells me that he will admit me, and off he goes. I feel relief with the sense that he is now in charge. He is the chief internist. I hear him tell the ER doc that there is only one bed left and that he will try to convince them to give it to me. Ten minutes pass. Twenty minutes.

The ER doctor returns. "There are no beds left in the hospital. We are going to have to transfer you," he says. I remain calm. I don't care at that point. I'm just happy I'm not roaming around Mumbai by myself. Apparently, Dr. Jain has some pull because a man in white eventually shows up with a wheelchair to take me to my room.

~~~

"In India, expect the unexpected." Dan read that quote in one of the many India books we perused prior to setting out for the mysterious subcontinent. There is the unexpected, and there is the unexpected. Life is an eternal present moment—an eternal now—from which we arise. There is simply one long stretch of eternity that we humans break down into bits.

Nothing is certain except death and the fact that everything changes. Yet we live our lives from one day to the next with some level of habituation, and the days become fairly predictable—that is, until the absolutely unexpected occurs. Be careful what you wish for. If you tell life you are ready to surrender, then life will ask this of you. It will test you again and again to provide you every opportunity to do so.

I *had* told life that I surrender. I shouted it loudly, in fact, inside of my head. No one else would have heard it but it was loud and clear to me. This happened during my first Vipassana meditation course. I was twenty-eight years old and about to break off the five-year relationship with the wild, fun-loving Australian man who'd become my fiancé. With reckless abandon we sold everything and moved to Hawaii. Just before the move, he asked me to marry him. I said yes. What I meant was no, but I was too busy evading the truth to be honest with him, or with myself for that matter. Because I was walking down a path with him that was not in alignment with my truth, I'd become depressed. My light had dulled. A waxy film had collected over the clear, shiny glass that was my looking glass. I turned even further from the truth, which was patiently knocking on my door. The light of it was so bright I needed sunglasses, but I couldn't bear to open the door and peer into it.

Charlie and I had come to a fork in the road. Charlie was the life of the party—the exuberant, adventurous, passionate life of the party. When I met him at the age of twenty-three, I loved the party. But as I slipped into my later twenties, it became apparent that it wasn't what I wanted anymore. That life didn't suit me even though I loved him a great deal. I thought the feelings of discontent—with him, our relationship, the endless nights of entertaining—meant something was wrong with me. I just hadn't yet owned up to the fact that the relationship was no longer serving me. It was that simple.

I had a dream while Charlie and I were together that I was trying to swim upstream against the current of a large, powerful, muddy river. I could hear the roar of the murky water. I struggled furiously to swim upstream against the current because there was a massive waterfall just downstream. I swam with all the force I could muster, but eventually the water was too strong, and I awoke as I was being swept over the falls.

Just before the move to Hawaii, we took our last annual May camping trip to the Canyonlands area of Utah. During our last night there while staying with Charlie's friend in Moab, Utah, I met his friend's wife Michelle who introduced me to the word *vipassana* and the idea of a ten-day silent meditation course. I knew right away I would attend. I'd actually started meditating a year earlier at the recommendation of a therapist who I was seeing in Boulder. The therapist taught me meditation 101 in her office.

"I don't have time for it," I told her.

"You don't have time not to," she replied.

When Charlie and I left for Hawaii, I had the sense I was strapped in a rollercoaster headed downhill, fast. My light at the end of the tunnel was the meditation course. I knew that if I could just get there I would be okay. I knew it. Six months after we moved to Hawaii I moved out of our place and into a house shared by two other women that was just down the street. I left for my first Vipassana course in Washington State shortly thereafter.

The silence was the easy part. I reveled in it. The first three days of the meditation course were spent entirely focused on the breath—the inhale, the exhale. After three days of silence and trying to keep my attention—my awareness—focused on my breath, continually bringing it back from the quagmire of conversation and drama-filled thought inside of my head to the breath, something gave inside of me. A dam cracked, a levee broke. I began to weep, silently weep. It was a deep cry, a purge, and it went on for three straight days. It was ancient sadness. As soon as I thought I had it under control, that I was finished crying, the wellspring sprung again. It was a deluge of sadness that sprung out of me like a geyser. I'd tapped into something old that had been buried deep inside of me for years and years. I knew then that there was something to this meditation.

It was early fall in Washington and there was fog and rain and the occasional deep-bellied howl of coyotes in the evening. In silence I ate. In silence I walked. In silence I looked upon the green earth as my being welled with a new perspective and my mind slowed down with each passing day. I smelled the grass, the air, the wetness that blanketed the earth like a placenta—one in which *everything* germinates. As the days went on and I slowed down more and more on the inside, the smells grew sweeter. Occasionally the sun peaked through the clouds and out in the distance stood Mount

Rainer as if to say, "Yes. Yes. Keep walking." It reminded me of a passage by Rumi: "Keep walking though there is no place to get to. Don't try to see through the distances, that's not for human beings. Move, but not the way fear makes you move."

On day four we were instructed in the technique of Vipassana meditation. During the instruction, which seemed to go on and on even though it only lasted about ninety minutes, we were asked to remain perfectly still. It became clear to me during what were likely the most physically excruciating moments of my life thus far—as clear as Mount Rainer through parted fog—that I was trodding my path. The physical pain I experienced became unbearable as the moments dragged on, and I resisted. It was then that I realized I had resisted discomfort for twenty-eight years. But the stubborn Aries determination inside of me wouldn't allow me to give up, even when the physical pain grew insufferable, when it felt like my hip joints were being ripped out of their sockets. I remained perfectly still and kept observing the pain.

Then some wisdom arose from the vast, still place inside that I'd started to experience. I went from being in pain—in agony—to observing pain. And it no longer hurt. I was in total equanimity with the pain for the first time in my entire human life. I became a silent witness to what was occurring inside of my body. This place from which I was able to observe the pain was neutral and still. There was space, immense space, between it and the pain. All became quiet. Vast. Like the sky bearing witness to slowly drifting clouds. The clouds drifting, the stuff of the clouds themselves—all neutral. I'm the one who assigns meaning to it, I saw clearly. The suffering became something I was merely observing, even if it was me who was suffering. It was and it wasn't. And the suffering was no longer suffering.

I was moved beyond words by what I experienced and there were more tears. It was then that I surrendered. I surrendered to the Truth that I experienced in the still, vast space that stretched out eternally before me, within me, that ultimately I would come to discover *is* me. *Is* all of us. I experienced the way in which my mind creates my suffering, and what it means not to react to it. Not to become or be the suffering. I returned to Hawaii after my first Vipassana course a woman forever changed. Six months later I left Hawaii, alone, and returned to Colorado.

I'm clear that I'm but a thread woven into an eternal tapestry. That which defines me, my borders, are ever morphing in response to my growth, my transformation, and the larger tapestry. One day I might fit neatly into a certain part of the tapestry, and then a few weeks, months, or years later either I've morphed or the collective has morphed, so I no longer fit where I once did. That's when it is time to move on. If it no longer resonates, it's not serving me. And it isn't good, bad, right, or wrong. It simply is. It's easy for me to overanalyze or condemn something that doesn't work for me. But really, it's just that the fit isn't a good one anymore. As Dan, my beautiful, brilliant husband, likes to say, "Life is way too short to wear uncomfortable shoes." Amen to that.

~

I think India heard that utter of surrender. She's an ancient place. I think of her as a mother. She is a wise teacher who uses tough love to show us who we are and what we are made of. She cracks us open, breaks us, so that our inconsistencies, our falsehoods, can come flowing out of us like yolk from an egg. And what is left—the space, the truth—can become our reality if we let it. She is the mirror of all mirrors. "Who are you?" she begs to know.

I have a friend who took to the world and began her travels at the ripe young age of eighteen. She was raped by four men in Athens, Greece. Afterward she began to have a recurring dream that her arms disappeared, and she knew instinctually that she had to find them before she returned to the United States. She realized that her arms were in India. She traveled to India and became very involved with the party scene in Goa. She developed a heroin habit. Eventually she met a Parisian and he became her travel partner. He, too, had the heroin habit.

She awoke one morning in Varanasi to find him gone, along with her passport, her money, a gold necklace given to her by her father, and anything else of value she had with her. After she lost everything—including her dignity—she crawled down to the Ghats of the Ganges River in Varanasi, sick from the heroin and weighing in at approximately ninety-five pounds. She called out to the universe, to God, and she let it be known that if she was to go on living she needed a sign.

Her gaze settled on the brown, murky water of the river that held the ashes of countless souls who no longer take the breath of life. It was then that she spotted the river dolphins—endangered freshwater dolphins whose eyes have no lenses and who use echolocation to navigate—breaching out of the Ganga. She knew deep down in the raw, bleeding place in her heart that she would make it.

The River Ganges, or Ganga, is believed to be the holiest river in India, and bathing in it is believed to purify the soul. Every day over sixty thousand people come to the Ganga to pray. Families of the dead travel many miles on foot, carrying the bodies of their deceased loved ones to be cremated in Varanasi. The ashes are then placed in the river. It is said that the cremation fires have been burning continuously for centuries.

As if on cue, a Danish woman appeared and took my friend in. Every morning for weeks the Dane would bring her a bowl of soup, nursing her slowly back to health—back from the clutches of death to the realm of the living. My friend noticed that there was a man in overalls who always walked several paces behind the Danish woman.

"Who is the guy in the overalls?" my friend asked when she had come through the post-heroin delirium.

"My dead husband," the Danish woman replied.

Eventually the Danish woman helped her buy a ticket back to the States. At the age of eighteen she had walked a fragile line between life and death and had been forced to choose between the two. India gave her both of her arms back so that she could go on living.

5

After my first night in the hospital, I watch the sky from the glass door in my room that opens to a balcony connecting all the rooms on my floor. The sky turns from black to gray, the first sign that Earth has completed its orbit and the sun's rays have returned to Mumbai. This light is something I desperately need. From this door in my hospital room, I look out over a little sliver of the Arabian Sea between two dilapidated hospital buildings in the foreground. There are sharp rocks that jut out of the water and the waves crash upon them. This scene is my refuge during my eleven-day hospital stay. Sometimes the water is rough and the waves lash the rocks with a fury I understand. Other times it is as calm as the breezes blown all the way from Africa that glide gently over its surface.

There is a wire strung between the two dilapidated buildings. Birds use it as a resting place from the currents of the wind and the water. There are two green parrots that spend hours resting on that wire every day. In India, parrots can be used to forecast the destiny of people. These parrots become symbols of hope for me. Sometimes they stare out at the sea with their backs to me, and sometimes they face me. I imagine they are looking in on me. I begin to get the feeling they might actually be my deceased maternal grandparents, Granny and Pop-Pop, who are here to convey a sense of security. *Is it you?* I ask them in my heart. It *feels* like it is. Granny and Pop-Pop were a second set of parents to my siblings and me. I would do anything right now to be rocked in the rocking chair by Granny, my head resting on her round belly and bosom, feeling her deep all-belly laugh.

Granny always liked to say, "Everyone, *remaaaaaiiiiiiin* calm," remain being said as a three-syllable word. I believe she said this more for herself than anyone else, but now it seems like a rather appropriate thing to say. I knew that the thought of me—her precious grandchild—traveling to India would be a burden on her soul. She'd worry herself sick. In Lynchburg, Virginia, where I spent my childhood, people didn't often go to places like India. They went to Europe, to Canada, to the Outer Banks of North Carolina, but largely they didn't travel to developing countries. With the exception of one doctor who traveled to Nepal to perform surgery on children with cleft palates, I didn't know anyone from Lynchburg who traveled to such faraway places when I was growing up. But I had a mother who not only gave me roots, but also gave me the strength and freedom of my wings. She allowed me to fly wherever the wind might take me, and so that is just what I eventually did, much to my Granny's dismay. From the time I was twenty-three and moved to Colorado, Granny encouraged me to move back to the East Coast. I think she thought I'd have a better chance of settling down with a nice doctor (like she did) if I made it safely back to Virginia. When I began meditating, she wondered if I'd joined a cult. After that first meditation course she asked me if I'd shaved my head. As she lay dying she wanted to know if I'd accepted Jesus Christ as my savior. Back then I thought it was because she was worried about my life's path. But looking back on it, I believe she was curious about *my* life experience. *My* spirituality. What I'd discovered to be true in *my* heart.

"Granny, I think Jesus was an enlightened man and I absolutely believe his messages of love, forgiveness, and compassion. But no, I don't accept him as my savior." What I didn't say was, "Jesus pointed and they worshipped his finger." What I didn't have the heart to say to her was, "Granny, I don't think he'd want you to accept him as your savior, either. I think he'd want you to be the master of your destiny, of your salvation, and do your own inner work. Like he did." The man didn't spend forty days and nights meditating in the desert so that people would worship him. He was leading by example.

When I began to feel the rumblings of India stir in my soul, I wasn't sure how I'd break it to her. So I didn't mention it. And it never turned out to be an issue. She passed away before I'd managed to buy a ticket. If the parrots are Granny and Pop-Pop, I imagine they are sending me unconditional love and support. I'm pretty sure that when you die, you lose the "I told you so" mentality.

I scan my room in the soft quiet of the dim morning light. I marvel at how clean and modern it is. The floor is sparkling white and there is a porcelain sink in the corner by the door to the corridor. In the corner to my left on the opposite side of the room by the glass door to the balcony is a television. I turn it on for five minutes during my time in the hospital. I am moving through something that feels so overwhelming I cannot handle the stimulation of a television. A bedside commode has been strategically placed next to my bed, and with it is an aluminum bowl full of wet cotton balls. I thank God for the toilet paper I still have in my backpack.

I have placed a few essential items—toilet paper, travel clock, journal, water filter, money belt, and guidebook—on the shelf next to my bed. I also have Dan's old bus pass that I kept because the picture on it is so wonderful. It was taken several years earlier, before I knew him. His head is half-cocked. He is smiling widely, as if he is about to break into laughter. I pick it up and study it in the dim light. I begin to cry. Eventually the clock says six, then six thirty. There is a knock on the door.

"Come in," I say.

In walks an older gentleman dressed in starched white cotton pants with a white shirt to match. Over the left shirt pocket stitched in light blue is his name, K. Z. Gaikwad. Under this are the initials B.C.H., Breach Candy Hospital. Funny thing is, *I* am a nurse at BCH—Boulder Community Hospital, and I work on the cardiac floor, Three West. And here I am, now settled in room 325, on 3 North, in India, doing another kind of work altogether.

I guess Mr. Gaikwad to be in his late fifties with his white-gray hair and the wrinkles that frame his eyes when he smiles. He is one of the "boys"—the males who work on the floor. They range in age from twenty to sixty and perform any number of jobs such as food preparation, mopping floors, and emptying bedside commodes. They function as nursing assistant, janitor, and food service worker combined.

Mr. Gaikwad is so much more than that. He is smiling from ear to ear, carrying a tray that he places on my bedside table. It has tea, milk, a few cubes of sugar, and several tea biscuits. Drinking black tea is arguably my favorite pastime on the planet. If the world ever goes to hell around me, I hope to have a cup of milky, robust black tea in my hand. The British left their mark on India. At Breach Candy Hospital, tea is served at six thirty, eleven, and again at four in the afternoon. This suits me more than fine.

Still smiling, Mr. Gaikwad surveys the room.

"Water?" he asks.

"Yes." I nod. "I need water."

He returns with a pink plastic pitcher filled with water. My heart sinks because I need water, but there is no way I am going to drink *that* water. I have no idea where it has come from. And if it's straight from the tap it won't do. I have already been dealing with dysentery for more days than is humane. I certainly don't need to make matters worse.

"Thank you." I smile, sincerely appreciative of his efforts. He walks around my bed to the balcony door and he gazes out at the lightening sky for a moment. When he turns around he is beaming.

"Okay?" he asks, in what I detect is very limited English.

"Yes, sir," I reply. "I'm okay." Half head bob and he slips out.

I don't think I slept last night. My knees were too swollen and painful to lie on my side, and I am not a back sleeper. I also had a fever that wouldn't quit and had me soaking my sheets. I asked the night nurse for pain medication and when I asked her what it was she brought me she answered, "Tablet." Whatever it was, it wasn't working.

With the exception of the laboratory workers who came to draw my blood, I was not interrupted. I spent the night trying to get comfortable and trying to figure out how I was going to call home. Perhaps one of the doctors will be kind enough to make the call, I thought. Maybe they can e-mail my parents. Dan is en route back to Boulder, but it might be a few days before he checks e-mail. He has a thirty-six-hour layover in Bangkok, and once he reaches Los Angeles he'll have a twelve-hour layover before boarding a plane for Denver. He is not traveling with a cell phone. Eventually the night nurse came to take my vital signs. I was still febrile, otherwise okay … except for the fact that my knees had officially rendered me unable to walk.

"Loose motion?" she asked me.

"Loose motion?" I repeated, not exactly sure what she was talking about.

"Loose motion?" she inquired a second time, as if I had not heard her.

"Loose *motion*? I don't know what you mean."

She pointed to the bedside commode. "Loose motion," she repeated, patiently. "Ohhhhhhhh … *loose motion*." It all has to sound so pleasant. Mark of the Brits, for sure.

Why yes, actually. I did have loose motion several times and getting myself to the bedside commode was a massive feat. It was one of the more painful things I've ever done, as my knees didn't want to bend or bear weight. Somehow I managed to get myself to a standing position by physically picking up each leg and moving it to the side of the bed, and doing everything in my power not to scream out in pain when I had to bend my knees over the side. Hanging on to the side rail on the bed, and using the armrests on the bedside john, I managed to move myself to the commode. If I'd been my nurse, I would've called myself a "fall risk" for sure. And had I (the nurse) known that I (the patient) was getting out of bed by myself without calling for help, I would've put a bed alarm in place. That would mean that every time I got up unassisted, a terrible screeching alarm would sound. But I'm not my nurse, and it was the middle of the night in Mumbai, India.

As I'm sipping my tea, watching the sun's rays find their way to the Arabian Sea, it dawns on me that I had seen a paragraph in my guidebook about the American Embassy in Mumbai. I'm not one hundred percent certain about the role of the embassy, but I have a feeling that they might be able to help. I patiently wait until they open to make the call. In the meantime, Mr. Gaikwad brings me a breakfast tray with a bowl of porridge and a hard-boiled egg.

"Okay?" he asks.

"Okay," I repeat, smiling back at him. I force myself to eat a little even though I'm not hungry. Dysentery does that to you. He returns thirty minutes later and the tray is largely still intact. He points at it with a look of dismay. This man really cares about me.

"I can't eat anymore. I'm just not hungry," I declare. He studies me for a moment. I think he wants to tell me that I need to eat more, but he doesn't know how to in English.

"Finished?" he finally inquires after a moment.

"Yes, sir," I reply.

"Yes, sir," he repeats, emphatically, grinning from ear to ear.

The day begins in full swing around eight thirty. My nurse, Ardi, arrives and looks me over. She checks my vital signs.

"Loose motion?"

"None since last night," I reply. She hands me some pills. "What are these?" I ask.

"Tablets," she replies.

"What tablets?" I ask, pressing further.

She studies me for a moment before answering. Most of them I have never heard of, but I do manage to glean that one of them is an anti-inflammatory, one of them is for fever, and one is a combination of an antibiotic and probiotic.

"Do you want sponge?" she asks.

"*Sponge?*"

"Yes, sponge," she repeats patiently.

"I'm sorry but I'm not sure what you mean," I finally admit.

"Bath," she states.

"*Ohhhhhh … sponge bath,*" I exclaim, finally understanding. "No, thanks," I go on. "I took a shower last night before I came in."

"Would you like to put on pajamas?" she asks. I am still wearing the clothes I came in with.

"That would be wonderful, Ardi."

And thus I am given my uniform—soft cotton pajamas that are blue-and-white checked, the top a short-sleeve button down, and the pants with a nice drawstring waist, my favorite kind. I am grateful for Ardi's easy and carefree manner.

"Are you married?" she asks.

"Yes, I am," I reply.

"Where is your husband?" she inquires further.

"He is on his way back to the U.S.," I explain. I can see that she is trying to make sense of the fact that I am in the hospital in the condition I am in while my husband is on his way back home. I begin to explain that he didn't, in fact, leave me stranded, but I don't have the energy to go into the details.

"I'm not yet married, but my parents are looking," she tells me. Ardi wears a starched white uniform, a short-sleeved dress that falls mid-calf. She has a white cap on her neatly kept short hair. She is attractive and confident. Her brown skin is soft and smooth.

Behind her enters a "boy" carrying a mop, also in a starched white uniform. They exchange a few words in Hindi and he begins mopping my floor, smiling at me the entire time.

"Air conditioner," he states smilingly, pointing at the temperature gauge on the unit above the glass door. Mumbai is a warm, muggy place, but I run cold so I had it off all night. He takes it upon himself to turn it on.

"I'll come back to start an IV," Ardi informs me. "You'll be receiving antibiotics."

She studies the contents on my shelf before giving me a warm smile and leaving the room. It's nine o'clock, so I dial the embassy.

"American Embassy," a friendly voice answers.

"Hi. I'm an American citizen and I'm at Breach Candy Hospital. I have no way of getting in touch with my family. Can you help me?"

"I'll transfer you to the American Civil Services Unit. Christy will be able to help you," the polite voice says.

I hold for a moment and a bubbly voice picks up. "Hi, this is Christy with the American Civil Service Unit. What can I do for you?"

"Hi, Christy. I'm Molly. I'm at Breach Candy Hospital. I can't walk, and I have no way of getting in touch with my family. If I give you the e-mail address of my parents and my husband, can you send them an e-mail?"

"Of course I can do that for you," she replies.

My mom checks her e-mail daily, and always first thing in the morning. I know that she'll receive the e-mail with my whereabouts and the phone number to my room when she wakes, which will be later in the afternoon Mumbai time. There is a massive sense of relief knowing that soon someone in my family is going to know where I am.

I grow sleepy once the relief begins to settle in. I'd like to nap but am swarmed by doctors. First there is Dr. Jain, who I'm happy to see again. He is accompanied by Dr. Vibha.

"How are you feeling this morning?" Dr. Jain inquires.

"I'm okay." Massive overstatement. I can't walk. Both knees are red, hot, and swollen, and the right knee is still growing in size. I can't bear weight. It is a major ordeal for me to get to the bedside commode. I didn't sleep last night. I'm scared. And I'm alone in India. *I'm okay* is my attempt to convince myself that I am not falling apart.

"This is Dr. Vibha," Dr. Jain says. "She will also be looking in on you." Dr. Vibha is in her mid-to-late twenties and looks like an angel. Her presence is soothing. Her features are soft and beautiful. Her long dark hair is braided neatly and her light blue *salwar kameez* billows out from under her white lab coat. Her slight frame stands tall with an air of confidence not found in many her age. When she smiles, there is light in her eyes.

With his stethoscope Dr. Jain listens to my lungs and my belly, and asks me about loose motion. Then he examines my knees.

"I am going to have an orthopedic surgeon take a look at your knees to see if we should drain them," he informs me.

They begin to flip through my chart and discuss my lab values.

"What is her white count?" Dr. Jain asks Dr. Vibha.

"It's elevated," she replies.

"What is it?" I inquire, wishing to be kept in the loop. They both look at me, slightly taken back.

"It's fifteen thousand," Dr. Vibha answers.

I have an infection. This is not news to me, but hearing it out loud, sidled with being alone in India unable to walk, is cause for concern. I hear something about my sed rate being elevated. An elevated sedimentation rate is an indicator of inflammation.

"What is my sed rate?" I ask. Again, they both look at me, curiously.

"Slightly elevated at forty," she says.

"What is her C reactive protein?" Dr. Jain asks of Dr. Vibha. C reactive protein is another indicator of inflammation.

"Quite elevated. It's a hundred." Normal is less than ten.

"Jesus," I say to myself.

"Have we sent a stool sample?" he asks her.

"I have ordered one," she replies.

"Will you check for *C. diff*?" I inquire. *C. diff* is *Clostridium difficile,* a diarrheal infection of the intestinal tract that can occur especially after antibiotic use when the normal bacterial environment in the gut is altered. It leads to the kind of diarrhea I am now having.

They both study me. "How do you know all of this?" Dr. Jain asks.

"I am a nurse," I reply.

"Make sure they check for *C. diff*," he instructs Dr. Vibha.

It becomes evident during my stay at Breach Candy Hospital that the culture of medicine in India is what it was in the U.S. back in the 1950s when nurses were subservient to doctors. In India, doctors are not used to being questioned, especially by their patients. Patients are not as informed as they are in the States. Nurses in India are responsible for far less than we are back in the states. It is also evident that they are not very respected. Earlier in our travels an Indian man told me that his nurse sister makes the equivalent of sixty cents a day.

My questions don't seem to bother Dr. Jain or Dr. Vibha; they are simply surprised by my direct and inquiring nature. After a few more moments, during which time they inform me that I am going to be started on IV antibiotics, I am left alone.

Twenty minutes pass and there is another knock on the door. In walks the assistant orthopedic surgeon. He is a young man in his mid-thirties. He introduces himself to me, hardly making eye contact, and throws the covers off my legs. I have my knees elevated on a pillow, as that is the only way I can obtain any relief from the pain.

"You cannot have these pillows under your knees," he declares as he yanks them out from under my legs. "You could develop contractures." Pain sears through my knees and I grab the sheet as I stifle a loud moan. "Don't worry about the pain," he adds. "I need you to bend your knees."

Don't worry about the pain? Clearly this guy has never experienced any pain in his life. Or his mind wandered during the part of the self-realization process where empathy and compassion toward others finally sets in.

"I need to see you bend your knees," he repeats.

I cradle my right knee in both of my hands and slowly begin to pick it up off of the bed. Dr. No Compassion impatiently grabs my leg, one hand under my foot and one hand under my knee. He starts to bend and straighten it. I am practically screaming by this point, writhing, as I clutch the sides of the bed. He is not even fazed. He repeats this with my left leg as I fight tears. I'm not sure why I don't punch this mother fucker, or at the very least order him out of my room.

"I'm going to order an X-ray of your knees," he says dryly. With that he leaves.

The pain is a 12 on a 1–10 scale, and whatever medication I'm taking for it isn't touching it. My positive attitude deteriorates. I look out of my little glass door at the sunny day outside, at the green water of the Arabian Sea, at the birds soaring in the currents above the water. Is this really happening to me?

I try to observe the searing sharpness in my knees, attempting not to spiral down into a bleak void that I sense lurks close by. I think of Dan, my mom, and the tears begin again. I close my eyes and try to focus my awareness on my breath. More tears. I write in my journal, trying to convince myself of all the wonderful things that will come of this experience such as greater strength and capacity, more awareness of the struggles of others. I only half believe it.

"Fuck," I say, over and over, as I struggle my way to the edge of the bed and onto the bedside commode, succumbing to another round of explosive diarrhea. Far be it for me to call for assistance. Once settled back in bed, I press my call bell. In walks Mr. Gaikwad, grinning from ear to ear. He has in his hands the tea tray with my eleven o'clock tea, milk, sugar, and tea biscuits. He places it down on my bedside table and walks over to the glass door. He points outside to the sky.

"God is great!" he declares.

Then he walks over to the bedside commode, picks it up as if it were a pile of dirty laundry, and leaves. My heart softens. Later he returns with a sparkly clean commode. He points to the tea tray.

"Finished?" he asks.

"Yes, sir," I answer.

"Yes, sir," he repeats.

I want to take him home with me, this sweet man who can't stop smiling at me even though he has to deal with my stinking diarrhea. And yes, Mr. Gaikwad, God is great. The entirety of that long stretch of vast eternal love is very great indeed. And it is in the simplest of moments that this greatness shows up. Thank you, Mr. Gaikwad, for your compassion and warmth. Thank you for showing me your greatness and a glimmer of that eternal love.

My IV is started before lunch and the first round of antibiotics is started shortly thereafter. I spend the rest of the afternoon unsuccessfully trying to sleep, writing in my journal, and attempting to meditate. My mind won't quit and I don't seem to have the diligence to keep at it. Agitated is an understatement for how I'm feeling. I move from feeling grateful for being alive, for being cared for by such sincere people, into moments of despair, like day moves into night, subtle shades growing darker and darker until the light has been swallowed completely.

I still don't know exactly what is happening inside my body. I only know that it isn't good. I recently heard about a yoga teacher from Hawaii who, while traveling in India, scraped her leg while riding a moped. The scrape became infected. She died from septicemia in an Indian hospital.

~

For the seventeenth time I try to nap, but there is a knock-knock-knock on the door.

"Come in," I call out.

A young woman who is about my age with a friendly smile and shoulder-length blonde hair peeks around the corner. She is very pretty in the all-American-girl way. She is wearing American-looking business attire.

"Hi, I'm Christy from the American Embassy." She extends her hand in a firm handshake.

Relief. I feel relief because of this human being in front of me. With that relief comes more tears.

"I'm Molly. It's really nice to meet you. Thank you so much for coming to see me." I wasn't expecting a courtesy call.

"You are certainly welcome. I was able to get your e-mails off earlier, so hopefully you'll hear from someone soon. The embassy is only a few blocks from here. I wanted to check in on you and see how you're doing."

"I'm hanging in there. It's nice to know that I'm not *totally* alone here, that someone actually knows where I am. Would you like to sit down?" I ask, pointing to a chair against the wall facing the glass door and the Arabian Sea beyond.

Christy takes a seat and begins to tell me a little about herself. She is from the Midwest—Norman, Oklahoma, to be exact. She is as friendly as everyone I have ever met from the Midwest. She and her husband have recently arrived in India. I am her first case at the embassy.

"How do you like India?" I ask.

"Well, it's different. Before India, my husband and I were stationed in Yerevan, Armenia. India is definitely different, but we're getting used to it. The people are so warm, and the colors and smells and sounds keep things interesting, to say the least. We have a pretty decent apartment, too. So things seem pretty normal here for us."

We exchange stories. I read concern for me in her face. I'm a woman her age, unable to walk, alone in a hospital room in Mumbai. The phone next to my bed rings.

"Excuse me, Christy."

"Hello," I say, hoping to God it's going to be my mom on the other end.

"Boodle?" I hear her soft, familiar voice. More big wet tears find their path down my cheek.

"Christy, it's my mom. Thanks so much for helping me," I say.

Christy stands to leave. "Is there anything you need?"

I pause for a second. "This seems a little above and beyond the call of duty, but I need toilet paper. I am almost out and they are giving me cotton balls to use instead. And I could really use a Coke."

"No problem. I'll bring them to you later when we head out to dinner."

"Thanks so much, Christy." She leaves, closing the door behind her.

"Mom, are you still there?"

"Molly, what happened?" she asks, the anxiety evident in her voice. I visualize the expression on her face, her furrowed brow, her soft brown eyes. My mother is a beautiful woman. It hurts my heart to know she has to endure the stress of my situation.

I launch into the story, play by play, beginning with my knees aching after Dan's and my overnight train ride back to Chennai from our honeymoon in the south. She listens patiently. After she is completely up to date, she asks me if I need her to come.

"No, Mom. I'll be okay. If I need Dan to come back, he will, but I know I will be okay."

I say this, trying to reassure myself as much as I am trying to reassure my mom. Mom has been to Italy. Twenty-five years ago. Her passport has long since expired.

"I might be able to get some sort of rush on a passport due to your medical situation," she says.

She would do it, too. This I know. My dear mother has laid down her life for her kids. She would give us everything she has, even if it meant she would then have nothing. She would drop everything and get on a plane and travel alone to India. I convince her that I will be okay and that Dan will come for me if I need him to. I find out later that these days become some of the most trying in her life.

Mom has three gems in this world. They are my brother, my sister, and me. She has always been there for us. Whether it's helping one of us drive a U-Haul across the country, attending every important event we've ever had, the casseroles, the laundry, the packed lunches, the breakups, the encouragement, the nightly "Now I lay me down to sleep, I pray the Lord my soul to keep" for my entire childhood—she has been the cheering section, the one constant, always there, rain or shine. It's brutal knowing how much suffering and worry this situation causes her.

The difference this time, she will later tell me, is that she is unable to physically be here for me. She is unable to make it better. And this rips her heart out of her chest. And that breaks mine. She stops drinking her nightly beer and begins drinking a nightly chai instead. It becomes her vigil. She decides to drink a chai every night until I have returned home safely. Her nights grow long and restless.

6

The second night in the hospital is an endless one. Once again I don't sleep. I try to find a comfortable position in the bed, but there are none. I can't lie on my side because my knees are anomalously swollen. I ask for pain medication and am given something that contains ibuprofen. The docs are holding out on me with the narcotics, and I am far too polite to kick and scream about it.

Once my IV antibiotics are completed, I am left alone for the remainder of the evening. I receive a call from Laurie who is aghast to hear what has happened. Apparently, Mom was at a loss for what to do after we hung up, so she forwarded the e-mail from the embassy to my travel e-mail list, letting everyone know what had come to pass. Laurie received that e-mail.

"I see you triumphant in this, Molly," she says to me.

I hang on to that word for dear life because what lurks beyond, beneath, and around me is despair so great it threatens to envelop me entirely. I sense its presence hiding in the shadows of my room.

I lie in the darkness and feel my heart beat in my chest, feel it pulsing in my neck. My whole body seems to move rhythmically with it. After several hours of unsuccessful attempts at slumber, I experience strong heart palpitations and fluttering in my chest that goes on for some time. I become short of breath and break into a cold sweat. Since I'm a cardiac nurse, I wonder what exactly my heart is doing. I wonder if I'm having runs of a dangerous heart rhythm. I don't call the nurse to report it. It's true that nurses make the worst patients.

I wonder if I am going to die here. I open the door to that possibility in my heart. I mean, really open it. I enter and stand naked in front of it, facing it consciously for perhaps the first time in my life. I make eye contact with it. I've only ever glanced in its direction—peeked into that room, and just as quickly closed the door and walked away. I've had patients die. I was with my grandfather when he died. But even though I've witnessed death, I haven't ever *really* faced it.

I think about my family, my mom especially, and wonder who it would be harder for—them or me: them having to feel the pain knowing I took my last breaths in a hospital room in India without a hand to hold or the whisper of *I will always love you* in my ear, or me having to take my last breaths by myself, experiencing my consciousness unwinding from my body, alone, not having the opportunity to say goodbye.

I decide it would be harder for them. I decide this because in the sanctum of my heart I know that though this life will end, it is not the end. Death is a transformation, just like every other moment of our lives. There is nothing final about it. It is like going off to college but a little more permanent. With death, we move into a new place, a new way of being, but there is no coming back for a visit in this form. Just like we arrive into the body, into our mother's womb from a place that most of us cannot perceive, we move back out into that vast expanse of stillness. It is scary because we have to enter the unknown alone. There is no taking anyone on this journey with us. That passage is a solitary one.

The night drags on. I grow short of breath, yet this time it is the anxiety coupled with pain beyond the likes of which anyone should have to bear. I hear the words of Pop-Pop in a dream I'd had years earlier.

"Have faith," he said to me in that dream. "All you have to do is have faith."

My grandfather died when I was sixteen. He died at home in bed, and my entire family stood around him as he took his last breath. My Pop-Pop was one in a million. He was an obstetrician. He championed human rights. There is a story about him delivering an African American woman's baby in a hospital closet in the 1960s when African Americans were not allowed in that hospital. He was instrumental in getting the first public library to open in Lynchburg, Virginia. Prior to that there was only a private library where Caucasian people were allowed. He was a good man. He was a kind man. According to my mom, we got the best of him. He was strict as a parent, but as a grandparent he was all love. My brother, sister, and I eagerly waited for him to return home from work. We'd hear his old Mercedes pull into the driveway after a long day at the hospital and grow giddy with the anticipation of him walking in the door. Granny would have a large vat of spaghetti on the stove, but that wouldn't stop us from digging deep into his pockets to mine the treasure that was invariably there every time. It might be a gumball or a fireball, and the day's catch was always fresh from the local drug store, caught only moments before on his drive home. That simple act of love was woven into the stability of my foundation.

Pop-Pop was also a pianist. He played exquisitely and wrote his own songs. I recall sitting under the piano watching his foot work the pedal, and sitting next to him as his fingers danced about the keys. One of the highlights of my childhood is sitting on his lap, holiday after holiday, when he played the Christmas carols for their Christmas party.

In my dream I was alone with him, standing next to him as he lay on a table dying. His spirit rose out of his body. It stood next to me and said, "It's like diamonds in the sky." Then his spirit walked over to a spiral staircase that wound up to a ceiling beyond which I could see nothing. He ascended that staircase, and just as he was about to pass from the room into the ceiling above, he turned back to look at me. His dark brown eyes pierced into mine.

"Have faith," he said. "All you have to do is have faith."

He then ascended the rest of the staircase, disappearing into the ceiling above.

Hours pass. I am still sitting upright when first light appears in the sky over the Arabian Sea. I realize that my time in the hospital is actually similar to my experience at the meditation courses. During the courses there is an immense amount of suffering that arises from a lifetime of conditioning. The practice is to observe what arises, to simply remain equanimous with whatever is arising.

For example, if I don't like the way that something feels, or I don't like the way that someone acts, irritation or resistance may arise inside of me. It is a physical sensation that I experience. The old habit pattern is to react to this irritation, to turn into a snap-dragon, as my husband likes to call it, or to resist whatever it is that is causing my discomfort. If I observe the irritation or the physical discomfort, I become more of a neutral witness to the irritation arising within me. I find myself *not* actually suffering. Or suffering less. And causing less suffering for the other person who might have become the recipient of my reaction. Eventually the feeling of irritation or discomfort passes like a cloud in the sky. Clouds are going to pass through the sky. This is the nature of reality. I can choose to become them—become anger, irritation, sadness—or I can choose to observe these things as they move through. As I observe my suffering—be it physical or emotional—a transformation naturally occurs. And with it, wisdom and clarity arise. Meditation—the practice of disarming the mind—works if we do it.

I try this. I try to observe the stabbing pain, but it is so difficult. In the moment it is much easier to reject the pain—to react to it, to lash out at the world, at eternity, at whoever cares to listen—than to observe it. It's like trying to tame a wild, green stallion that tears out of the pen bucking, kicking, and galloping. It's not easy. And I suffer, big time.

Before dawn, my night nurse comes to take my vital signs. Loose motion only twice during the night, and yes, I have a fever. It never seems to matter how bleak, dark, and long the night is. Once the sun finds its way back to Mumbai and morning has birthed itself, everything shifts. I fill with hope and gratitude. That becomes the pattern during my stay at Breach Candy Hospital. Although the situation feels immensely heavy, there is a lightness woven into it. There is a knowing, a calm that arises with dawn. It is a visceral awareness that I'm a part of the all-that-is, that I am, in fact, arising from it.

I've been asking consciously to evolve since my late teens. I have been putting it out there in the form of prayers and intentions. Traditionally, they went something like this: "Help me be more tolerant, more kind, more caring, less judgmental. Help me be of service." Eventually my circuitous wanderings led me to Vipassana. It got my attention. Because of the meditation practice, I accessed a space I'd only ever glimpsed. Initially you don't get there and stay there. Well, maybe some do. It seems that more often there is a slow sinking in that happens. For an instant I experience Truth, am awakened to it. Eventually I'm sucked right back into my old ways, my old mental habit patterns—the aversion to things or situations that are uncomfortable, the need to control the outcome, to have things be certain when they never can be. Then I come up for air and once again experience Truth ... and I give importance to the practice that helps me stop reacting to life so I can experience the beautiful, brilliant present. Then I'm sucked under again by my currents, by the riptide of my mind— the old habit patterns, egoic structures—and Truth evades me and I find myself suffering. Again.

There is a brilliant poem written by the late poet Portia Nelson. It illustrates clearly the progression out of these various habit patterns. It is entitled "Autobiography in Five Short Chapters." It outlines a journey walking down a street and encountering a deep hole. Initially she falls into the deep hole, a victim to it. Over the course of the five chapters she goes from walking down the street and not seeing the hole and falling in, to seeing the hole and still falling in, but taking responsibility for it. Eventually she walks down the street and avoids the deep hole. By chapter five she chooses to walk down another street altogether.

I suppose if you want to stop a gal in her tracks, slow her down, force her to surrender to the fact that *everything* really is arising and passing away like clouds moving through the sky, you could just render her unable to walk in a foreign country where she doesn't have the comforts of anything familiar around her. That'll get her attention.

Mr. Gaikwad's face appears at my door; he's smiling from ear to ear. He pushes open the door with his body and enters, placing the tray of tea and biscuits on the bedside table. He points outside to the sky, and his smile widens even further over his face. "God is Great!" he declares. I smile back at him and my heart breaks open a little.

Ardi enters after I have eaten my breakfast.

"Sponge today?" she inquires.

"Yes, Ardi, I'll have a sponge today. But I can do it. I just need some water and a washcloth." She pokes her head out of the door and says a few words to someone in the hall. In a few moments Mr. Gaikwad appears with a large basin of steaming hot water and a towel slung over his shoulder. He leaves and hurries back a moment later with clean sheets.

"I am going to change your bed while you wash," Ardi informs me.

"That's fine, Ardi, but I'd like to sit at the side of the bed while you do that."

Half head bob in response.

It takes time to maneuver my legs to the side of the bed, much like cautiously handling dynamite. I do my best to breathe through it. Once I am seated on the side of the bed I shyly remove my hospital pajama top and wash my arms, my pits, and my torso with the steaming water while Ardi starts changing the bed on the opposite side. I slip the clean top on and remove the pajama bottoms, letting them fall to the floor. I wash my lower half and dry off with the clean towel, managing to slip the clean bottoms over my feet without standing. Eventually I am forced to stand, holding onto the bedside table for dear life so I can pull up the pants and Ardi can finish making the bed. I'm not steady on my feet and the pain immediately tears through my knees.

"Anything else?" Ardi asks when we're finished.

"Could you please hand me my toothbrush?"

So this is what it feels like to be dependent on others. It has always been difficult for me to ask for help, though I'd bend over backwards to help someone else. I learned early on to be self-sufficient and to take care of others but never felt comfortable allowing others to take care of me. I've been taking care of patients as a nurse for years now and am finally on the other side of the bed sheet. For some in this life, it is more comfortable to give, and for some it is more comfortable to receive. While one is not better or worse, it is helpful to learn to do both.

A little later there is a knock-knock on the door and Dr. No Compassion walks in. Busted. I am *so* busted. Once again, with an aloof hello he tosses the covers off of me.

"Like I said yesterday, you cannot have these pillows under your knees." He takes them out from under my knees, this time a little more considerately. He picks up my knees, one by one, and takes them through the vitriolic exercise that he did yesterday. I am in a cold sweat and beginning to feel nauseous from the sharp pain. My eyes tear, but I'll be damned if I am going to let this man see me cry. I bear it.

"You've never done yoga, have you?" I ask mordantly.

"No," he answers.

"I didn't think so. In the practice of yoga you move to your edge slowly. You don't race to your edge and then try to go beyond it." He gives me a blank stare as he continues exercising my knee.

"We will look at your knees tomorrow and decide then if we are going to drain them." With that he is gone.

Moments later Dr. Vibha appears, her soft gentle nature in stark contrast to her colleague's arrogant, callous manner.

"How are you this morning?" she asks.

"I think I am okay."

"Loose motion last night?"

"Twice."

"Let me look at your knees."

She gently places her hand on my knees one at a time.

"They are warm," she says.

"I know," I reply.

"Your white blood cell count is up more today."

"What is it?"

"Twenty-four thousand."

"Jesus."

"We are still waiting on your blood cultures, but we are going to start another IV antibiotic."

"Fine. And Dr. Vibha, that orthopedic doctor is very rude. He inflicts serious pain on me every time he comes in here. I don't want to work with him again." Yes, I am firing the callous Indian doctor.

"I encourage you to speak to Dr. Jain about it," she says. By the way she says this, with a hint of a grin behind her attempt to be serious, I can tell that *she* would love to see him fired as well. Apparently, this is not the first time this young doctor has been rude.

Moments later Dr. Jain arrives, placing his hand on my shoulder and peering deep into my eyes.

"How are you, Molly?' he asks with obvious concern.

"I am okay," I reply, forgetting to mention the excruciating pain or the fact that I haven't slept for the second night in a row. Somehow those things seem to lose their importance in the light of day.

"I am going to have the senior physician in the hospital see you today. His name is Dr. Udwadia."

Either I am really sick or a very interesting case.

"Okay," I reply. "And Dr. Jain, may I *not* have that orthopedic doctor come see me again?"

"What has happened?" he asks.

"He inflicts intense pain on me every time he comes in here. And he is very impolite. I don't want to work with him anymore."

"Okay, okay, that is fine. I will see to it that he does not come in here again, and if necessary, we'll have a different orthopedic doctor visit you."

Not long after they leave, there is another knock-knock on the door. In walks a distinguished elderly doctor, followed by a coterie of younger interns. He is the kind of man who commands respect and obeisance by his presence alone. He walks into the room and I find myself straightening my spine and clearing my throat. The only other person I have ever met who had this effect on people was my high school A.P. English teacher, Dr. Locke. There is an air about these people; maybe they have so much respect for themselves that you are left with no other option than to follow suit.

Dr. Farook Udwadia is light skinned compared to most Indians. He is soft-spoken but heard. He looks at me from behind piercingly authoritative brown eyes.

"What is your story, child?" he asks. I *feel* like a child around him. I relay the details of my last month in India, including the two rounds of dysentery, the bilateral eye infection, and ending with my knees becoming large, round ruby red grapefruits that could no longer carry me.

"What is her white count?" he asks one of his interns, who is fumbling through my chart. A moment passes. No answer.

"Twenty-four thousand," I state. Dr. Udwadia turns and looks at me curiously. "What is her sed rate?" he asks. They are silent as the young intern flips through my chart.

"It was forty yesterday, but I believe it is up to sixty today," I say.

Dr. Udwadia looks at me again. I detect the slightest raise of one eyebrow, a gesture that my mom and sister have perfected. It's a gesture that is either curious or curiously disapproving. Patients are not routinely part of their care here. And I am a woman. I believe the interns are slightly amused. I can see this by the small grins they are trying desperately to conceal as they eye me over.

"You have Reiter's syndrome," Dr. Udwadia states mat-ter-of-factly.

"I have what?"

"Reiter's syndrome."

"I have never heard of that," I say.

"Of course you haven't," he says, without a hint of condescension. "You are a Sister. You don't treat illness," he explains. Word has gotten out that I am a nurse. In India, nurses are referred to as Sisters, thanks to Mother Teresa and the large number of nuns who've ended up as nurses in this developing country.

I'm a little annoyed by what he said, but I decide it is probably better not to challenge him. He tells me that Reiter's syndrome is an autoimmune illness. It is also called reactive arthritis. These days it tends to be referred to as reactive arthritis, because Reiter was a German physician who was part of Hitler's Third Reich, so it's not considered politically correct to use his name.

Autoimmune illnesses run in my family. Those of us who were lucky enough to inherit the gene HLAB27 are predisposed to illnesses such as reactive arthritis, ulcerative colitis, and ankylosing spondylitis. There have been more than a few appearances of diseases of this nature within my family. Granny suffered from rheumatoid arthritis as well as ulcerative colitis *and* lupus.

Until now, I've never had any problems of this kind. In fact, I'd been unaware that I possessed the gene. There are five bacteria known to set off the inflammatory pathways that lead to reactive arthritis. They are *Shigella, Salmonella, Ursinia, Campylobacter,* and *Chlamydia.* Half of all travelers to the developing world will come down with diarrhea, and some of the aforementioned organisms could be responsible for its onset. Most of those who come down with this inconvenient weight-loss program will get over it just fine—maybe a little tougher for having gone through vomiting and shitting all day and night for days on end, not sure if they are going to live or die. But a small percentage of those unfortunate souls will go on to develop reactive arthritis.

It can affect any of the joints in the body, but it usually affects the large joints. Hence my knees, which have grown into the most massive joints that anyone has ever laid eyes upon. The prognosis is uncertain. Most people who develop reactive arthritis will improve back to their normal state of functioning within four to six months and may or may not ever go on to have other issues with it. But some of the weary souls who end up with it, usually those with the gene HLAB27, go on for months, or years, with the illness. If they do improve, which is not a guarantee, they may or may not return to their pre-illness state, and they could go on to have flare-ups in the future.

It's an inflammatory condition. Inflammation: flame, heat. Shortly before I left for India I was told by two alternative health care practitioners in Boulder that they detected intense amounts of heat—of fire (I *am* an Aries, fire sign extraordinaire)—in my body. It wasn't said as a compliment, but more as a warning. Too much of anything is not a good thing. I had lived "fast and furiously," as Granny always liked to tell me. "Slow down," I heard from her over and over. Heat is produced from rapid internal movement.

Then I chose nursing as a profession. The pace that one keeps inside of a hospital is totally insane. Nurses run all day long. You actually need to be everywhere at once. This leaves no time to eat or pee, much less sit for five minutes. And when things speed up, they heat up. It is a law of nature. As it is above, so it is below. If the mental state is hurried, it follows that the body might be affected.

As I developed in my meditation practice, and began to slow down from the inside out, there was definitely an internal struggle that began. When you slow down, truly slow down, you have to let go of things, pare down to what is essential. That was difficult for me, not being everything to everybody. Not being able to give as much face time to people as they might wish. I read somewhere that a Zen master once said, "Open your hand and let the dead wood drop."

I've heard it said that the gene is the loaded gun, and the environment pulls the trigger. Apparently, something in my internal environment is shifting itself. When the pendulum swings too far in one direction, it must swing back. We never know what that will look like.

Two more sleepless nights pass, accompanied by days filled with incredibly labile emotions. Profound clarity and peace morph into fear, desperation, and grief. It feels like I am riding a rollercoaster of emotion that is intensely working me, squeezing my insides as though I'm being ground through a meat press.

I write in my journal: "I have asked for nothing else for so long other than to evolve spiritually. Well, this is making it happen ... you surrender and realize that you only have right now. That is all. I created this."

The part about only having "right now"—it's something I was beginning to grasp on an intellectual level pre-meditation. But when I actually experienced it (because my mind quieted down enough to truly experience what the present moment is), everything changed for me. The present moment *is* all we ever have. Now *is* the divine. Heaven is here. And it's now.

I've experienced this immensity in flashes because my mind has been so busy, trying so hard, dissecting the past or planning the future. Trying to concretize life and make it fit my worldview. I've judged as negative that which I'm averse to or perhaps don't understand, instead of allowing it to simply be because it is.

Upon close observation it is apparent to me that my ego tries to morph things to fit *my* worldview. We don't all wear the same colored glasses. Our life experience determines the color of the filter through which we see and perceive the world. And since we've all had such massively different experiences, there is no way that we'd all perceive life the same way.

Just because something isn't my preference or I don't understand it doesn't mean I need to make it wrong or negative. Things are as they are, and this is every bit as neutral as a tree growing slightly curved to the left out of a need for sunlight or a weed that grows only in moist, shady climates because that is what suits its nature. It is far simpler to observe whatever reaction I might be having to what someone is saying or doing than to step in and try to alter things. It *feels* better. There is a sense of relief that comes with not needing to defend anything, to fix or change anything, even though the urge does still present itself. Out of that silent stillness that underlies everything arises immense freedom.

The now that is always here is teeming with the unconditional love, the unconditional support that my being is ultimately seeking. That my being ultimately is. I've been filled with judgment about how things should or shouldn't be, problem solving a situation that hasn't even arisen so therefore cannot be figured out. If I just relax and let life happen, there isn't a problem to solve. If I allow and trust, life unfolds in a natural, fluid way.

It was amazing to me when I began to observe the activity in my mind how much time I spend trying to figure out situations that haven't even occurred, wheels spinning about something that has happened in the past, or about some story I have going about someone or something, like a record player caught in the rut of the record, skipping and skipping and skipping. Usually, when I follow the mind down those paths, I create physical stress and a pile of tension. And that pile of tension works against my well-being.

It is much more freeing to let that all go (but difficult to do and takes massive commitment to achieve) and bring the awareness back to right now. Free that record player arm from that rut! Free my life from that rut!

Evolution is like peeling an onion. There are layers upon layers that are peeled off and the wisdom arises inversely. But just because I experience something, learn it on some level, doesn't mean I have mastered it. Apparently, I need to learn the lesson again (and again and again), in a much more visceral way. It's unlearning the learning—learning how not to react to life—to things, to people, to our-selves. Learning not to *be* the mental patterns that I put into place early on to survive. For while they once served me (or I would not have developed them), I no longer need them.

There are countless examples of reactions to external stimuli, to life, that people have, such as fear from contending with the unknown or anxiety about a certain situation. It is one thing to become aware of the reactions and say, "Ah, I am not going to react anymore." Putting it into practice takes heaps of practice, lifetimes some would say. Just because we decide to quit reacting doesn't mean those seeds of reaction inside of us that were planted and have taken root and have grown into big tall trees will automati-cally go away. It doesn't work like that. If it did, I'd be genuinely smiling through all of this. That's why monks and nuns give up layperson life.

Any moment we happen to be in is a culmination of all of the previous moments of our lives. It is the sum of all of the previous parts. Things aren't random. They don't happen haphazardly to us. We are not victims of life happening *to* us. Being alone and unable to walk in India is providing me with the perfect venue to lose con-trol and open to whatever is happening. It's a free-fall, actually. A wise acupuncturist I know who lived in India for eight years told me that when something goes wrong with your knees, it's all about your ego. Apparently, something in me said *bring it on*. I bow to you, O Ego of mine. I surrender.

~

Four sleepless nights has me utterly exhausted. In fact, I am so exhausted that I can't smile at anyone anymore. The knee pain as-sails, and I am sucked back into depths of despair. I am done. Com-pletely done. All I can do now is cry. I am crying when Mr. Gaikwad brings me my six thirty morning tea. I am still crying when he brings my breakfast tray at eight o'clock. I am crying when the nurse arrives with my tablets. I haven't touched my food.

"I don't want to have a sponge today," I declare.

Ardi looks at me with her head tilted, suspended in mid head bob, a slight frown on her face.

"Don't cry," she says, and with that she leaves.

Don't cry, I think to myself. I cry harder.

She returns with Maria, a seasoned veteran of a nurse who is in charge of the floor. Maria, who I nickname Mother Teresa, is soft and brown and buxom. Her being is so gentle that her skin exudes it. She is all heart. Her short, dark hair frames her face like a halo, and that combined with her starched white nurse's cap really do leave her looking like a Sister. She has checked in on me every day. She sees my tears and envelops me with her strong, sturdy arms. My face is smooshed into her bosom, and so now are the snot and the tears. She doesn't care. She strokes my hair and holds me, and eventually I get some sort of grip. Then Dr. Vibha walks in.

"What is the matter, Molly?" she inquires upon seeing me in such an emotionally distraught state.

What is the matter? I repeat to myself silently, surprised by the question because from my vantage point, I can't discern what *isn't* the matter. I'm unraveling. I am not in control. It is terrifying.

"What is the matter is that I'm alone, my family is thousands of miles away, and I can't walk. What is the matter is that I am in excruciating pain and I haven't slept for four nights. What is the matter is that I have some syndrome I don't know anything about."

I am now crying so fervently, my speech is made incoherent by heaving sobs.

"What is the matter," I say, catching my breath, "is that the only time I have been out of this bed for almost four days is to get myself up to the commode." I am in unchartered territory. I have absolutely no control over the situation. I am bearing witness to the person I have known as me my entire life totally unravel for the first time I can remember. I am not able to walk. I am totally reliant on strangers.

I don't know if I can swallow the situation whole. I do know, from somewhere in those dark, murky depths of my soul, that I really can swallow it whole; it's just that I know it's going to hurt like hell going down. I've always been a firm believer in the adage "You are never given a situation that you can't handle." I know I've got some serious staying power. It's just that I feel like kicking and screaming about it for a while.

Dr. Jain enters and takes a good look at my red, puffy eyes.

"What is the problem?" he asks in his gentle fashion. I repeat myself, although now I have started to calm a bit. He studies me for a moment.

"You are going to be okay." I almost completely believe him. He puts his hand on my shoulder, and staring into my eyes he says, "You must smile. If you are going to heal you must smile."

"She *has* been smiling," Mother Teresa says.

They all clear out except for Ardi. "I understand why you are upset," she says, putting her hand on my hand. She stands by my side quietly for a moment before leaving.

Later that afternoon I am speaking on the phone with Kat, a dear childhood friend. She is a friend with whom I share history, but we've also managed to evolve together as human beings.

She has become a champion for me as this situation unfolds. She is now living in Cambridge, England. She is threatening to board a plane for Mumbai, and I don't put it past her. I manage to convince her that Dan will be calling soon and that he will come for me if I need him to. She has called daily since receiving my mom's e-mail with words of strength and encouragement. Her words have become beacons of light for me. They carry me through the darkest hours of my life that I remember thus far. She has cast a safety net and I am suspended in it.

We are speaking on the phone after my big meltdown. She detects the shift in my voice that has occurred over the last couple of day. She detects the sadness and defeat that is setting in.

"I picked an angel card for you today, Mol. It reads: 'You'll be triumphant, and your desires will manifest. Any obstacles are temporary. ... Don't worry about the appearance of challenges because they are just an illusion that will soon disappear. If you worry excessively about these issues, you'll fuel them with power and energy. See them instead as wispy clouds that can't really block you. ...Your life is becoming more stable with a quieter form of excitement. The drama of obstacles is now a thing of the past.'"

I cling to the word *triumphant*. It's all I have—hope of being triumphant, whatever that looks like. I am speaking to Kat, the word *triumphant* echoing through the chambers of my heart, when Anish, my new physical therapist arrives, walker in hand. I learn that Dr. Jain and Dr. Vibha ordered physical therapy to begin when I first arrived in the hospital, but somehow the order was overlooked. Anish assures me we will not do anything I can't do but that it's time to get this old bag of bones moving. It has been four days since I was last mobile, with the exception of getting myself to the bedside commode and back again.

"Even after just a few days of immobilization," Anish says, "the deconditioning can have a profound impact on your functioning."

It is late afternoon. The quality of the light reflected off the water is different from the early-morning light. The water is choppy, little white caps breaking off of the rocks out in the distance. I inhale deeply, understanding what is before me.

Independently, Anish repeats the sentiments of Dr. Jain. "You must smile on the inside if you want to heal." These Indians fully comprehend the mind's role in the healing of the physical body.

The laboratory at Breach Candy Hospital has a quote painted on the wall: "If God answers your prayers, he is increasing your faith. If God delays, he is increasing your patience. If God doesn't answer at all, he knows you can handle it PERFECTLY."

"I want you to bend your knees, one at a time," Anish says. "We'll start with your right knee."

These are the preparatory exercises, the ones that will make my knees limber enough to get out of bed. That sounds simple enough. What I face, however, isn't simply a matter of bending my knees. I face the mass of fibrous inflammation and fluid that has completely inhabited the space where once only the structure of my knee joint lived. Bending them isn't as easy as it sounds. It requires that I sort of mow a pathway in the grass—the grass, the brush, being the fibrous mass of inflammation that has taken over like weeds gone wild.

I begin by lifting my right knee a fraction of an inch off of the bed. It's excruciating.

"Again," Anish repeats. "Again."

I repeat this over and over until I can lift the knee another inch off of the bed. And each time I incrementally raise the height of the knee bend, with intense pain I mow the pathway that much smoother, the fluid-filled fibrous resistance threatening to move back into its place and foil my efforts. After ten minutes, I have successfully been able to raise my knees more than a few inches off of the bed.

After several rounds of these painful repetitive exercises, it's time to get me walking. It takes two hands and everything I am made of to maneuver my knees, inch by agonizing inch, to the side of the bed where they can begin the long, arduous journey toward a ninety-degree angle. It's all up to Rightie and Leftie. Rightie seems to be having a more difficult time than Leftie. She's almost unable to bear any weight. Eventually they're both on the floor and I am erect, two hands on the walker, with Anish smiling patiently in front of me as I begin. Leftie and Rightie don't quite remember what they are supposed to do. I hesitate.

It's heel-toe, heel-toe, and remembering to take small steps, not big steps, because if you don't, you end up going too fast and not bending your knees at all, walking much like a penguin from side to side with little shuffling steps. All of a sudden the situation—the fact that I am very ill, contending with more pain than I have ever experienced in my life, alone in India, and learning how to walk at the age of thirty-two—seems so out of control that I start giggling. And the giggling opens me up just enough for a little light to get through to that heavy heart of mine.

We make it out into the corridor. I receive curious looks from Indians who are visiting their sick loved ones. Indians are the most curious people I have ever met. I am aware that it must be odd to see a young white woman, pale and dysentery ravaged, learning how to walk in her soft cotton light-blue-checked hospital pajamas. I feel a sense of freedom as it sinks in that I am thirty-two years old and learning to walk in India. It is liberating when you are forced to give up the control over your life that you never had in the first place.

At the end of the hall through an open window I see a large palm tree. I hear its fronds rustling against one another, and beyond there is the honking of horns, barely an audible din in my room. That eternal honking horn that makes India India has until now been a source of agitation. But I am hearing it with different ears now. It leaves me feeling less alone. It helps me feel that I am still a part of this life, which is reassuring, because using a walker to propel myself down the hall certainly does not feel compatible with the kind of life I am used to living.

As we slowly make our way back to my room, I tell Anish that one day I am going to write about all of this.

"I want a pen name. What is a good Indian name?" I ask, thinking it might be appropriate, since India is tearing me to pieces.

"Durga," he replies.

"I like that. Durga," I echo as we turn the corner and make our way back into room 325. Durga is a goddess associated with, among several things, war and battle. In Sanskrit, Durga means "the Inaccessible" or "the Invincible." This sounds about right since the experience at times feels like battle. A battle between what is happening to me and how I am responding to it. A battle between what life was for me and what it is for me now. A battle between what is happening and what I want to be happening. Ultimately, a battle between me and myself.

My slice of the Arabian Sea as seen from room 325

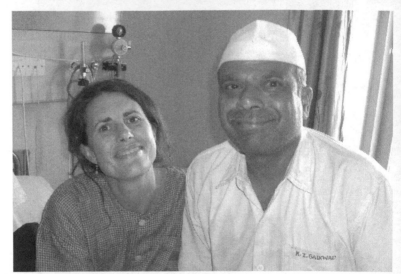

Mr. Gaikwad and me

From left, Maria (Mother Teresa), nurse, Dr. Vibha, Dr. Jain, me

Dr. Farook Udwadia

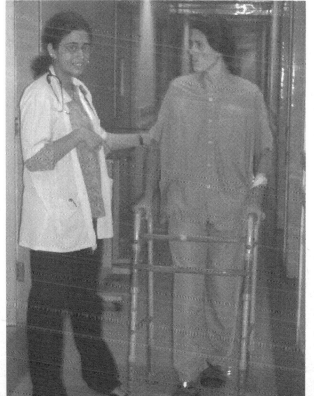

Walking at Breach Candy Hospital

part two

If you want to be whole,
Let yourself be partial.
If you want to become straight,
Let yourself be crooked.
If you want to become full,
Let yourself be empty.
If you want to be reborn,
Let yourself die.
If you want to be given everything,
Give everything up.

—Tao Te Ching

8

After a thirty-six-hour layover in Bangkok (that began just after renegade terrorists bombed the city with eight bombs) and a twelve-hour layover in Los Angeles on his way back to the U.S., Dan lands in Denver. He arrives home early in the morning and promptly goes to bed. Traveling to and from India is no small thing. After sleeping most of the day, he logs on to check his e-mail while checking phone messages. There are voicemails from our friends wanting to know how I am doing, as they all received the desperate e-mail from my mother. Eventually he gets to the urgent e-mails and text messages from Kat indicating that if he doesn't get on a plane bound for Mumbai, then she is going to. I've asked her if she thinks I might die here in Mumbai, and she is more than a little concerned about me. He calls, still in a fog from travel and sleep.

One ring, two rings.

I pick up, hoping desperately that it's Dan on the other end. "Hello."

"Molly?" he says, somewhat sleepily and confused about what is happening.

"*Dan.*"

As soon as I hear his voice, tension in my being releases and big fat tears fill my eyes. I update him on the events that have come to pass since we parted. And then I tell him that I am okay, that although I am in a hospital alone in India, in terrible pain and barely able to walk, I think I'll be able to manage without him coming back for me. *Enough of the tough girl act already. It is okay to need people. Especially your husband.*

When Dan and I were married, the song we chose to dance our commemorative dance to was a Dave Matthews song. It begins "I would travel halfway around the world just to sit down by your side." That is just what he did.

~~~~~

"Among the lucky you are the chosen one." That is what my fortune cookie told me two months earlier while I was eating dinner with Dan at Chez Thuy—one of my all-time favorite restaurants in Boulder. One might discount a fortune of this nature and say that my opening *that* particular fortune cookie on *that* particular night was a random event. But I do not believe in random, in happenstance, although entropy would suggest that the particles of the universe are moving toward chaos, disorder, that things are more desultory than not. No, there is cause and there is effect. Something cannot come from nothing. The pebbles that we drop into the water of our lives cause a rippling outward, without fail.

Two years prior to that fortune, I received one at the same restaurant that read, "Love is just around the corner." At that time I was thirty years old and longing to meet the man of my dreams. He was out there. I felt him. I was single after having broken off the engagement to Charlie a year and a half earlier. So the "Love is just around the corner" fortune was music to my ears.

I was ready for a partner who could comfortably reside with me in that still, silent space devoid of words—one who wanted to stay home on a Saturday night, light candles, and just *be*. I wanted a man who was exploring his inner landscape. One who experiences the presence of the Truth, the presence of something much greater than the "I" at the apparent level—the level seen with the eyes.

For God's sake, I survived my Saturn Returns intact, and maybe I felt a tad deserving of some good fortune. According to my astrologer friend Andrea, Charlie and I broke up right in time for my Saturn Returns. Andrea has been in Boulder since the 1970s. She loves art and Santa Fe, New Mexico. Santa Fe has a tendril that is loose and flowing and weaves itself into the heart of a certain type of person—the kind who gravitates to azure blue against desert red rock, to adobe, linen, and art. She reads the stars and the planets and deciphers their meaning with jaw-dropping accuracy.

After returning to Boulder from Hawaii, I yearned for solace in the form of an explanation for all that had come to pass in my life. Andrea and I were seated at a small round table in North Boulder. She began to explain the meaning of Saturn Returns. I listened, hungry to understand what I felt in my heart.

"Saturn Returns is an astrological phenomenon whereby the planet Saturn completes its cycle through your birth chart to the spot it occupied when you were born. It occurs between the ages of twenty-eight and thirty."

I gazed into her hazy, blue eyes, leaning intently into what she said.

She went on, "It is known to be a time of endings and new beginnings and can be a time of pain and turmoil. If in fact you have been living your truth, the fruits of your labor are reaped. If you aren't living in accordance with your true nature, you tend to make big changes during this time."

"That feels about right," I said.

"If you don't face these things during your first Saturn Returns," she said, "it'll be more difficult when you are fifty-eight and it happens a second time. We become more set in our ways. Saturn Returns is like a giant spring-cleaning. You let go of people, occupations, and things that no longer serve you. So, congratulations. Consider yourself lucky, sister." I believed Andrea that the truth was already in me somewhere, but I wasn't quite ready to hear it from myself.

It took me a long while to get over Charlie. I wasn't remotely interested in drowning my woes in casual sex. I dove into my meditation practice, hung out with my girlfriends, and told my journal the inner workings of my soul. One entry, dated a month before I met Dan, reads:

Move me that I may move
toward you.
Help me let go of weight,
of learned behavior.
Allow me to open,
that you may flow freely through me.
I give thanks to you, Spirit.

After a year and a half of singledom and austerity, I began to feel like a piece of ripe, succulent fruit ready to be picked from the tree and tasted, gently and deliberately. I knew what I wanted in a man. I was clear about that. I'd written letters in my journal to the divine, letting this presence know that I was indeed ready to meet my life partner, just in case there was any doubt in the matter. I'd been doing my inner work, and I was ready to find a partner who was also doing his inner work.

Four days before I laid eyes on that beautiful man I call my husband, my journal reads, "I am an open door right now, in the heart sense. I am ready, absolutely ready to share my life with my life partner. I am ready to grow with him, to be raw and vulnerable, to bear the deepest, deepest parts of my soul to him, the ones with cobwebs and dust."

I'd been told by three different people that this mystery man would be entering stage left. One woman revealed the actual month he would arrive. A nurse I worked with at the hospital quite correctly told me what he would look like, right down to his big green eyes. A palm reader at the Boulder Creek Festival indicated that I would travel and that he would be with me. Of course when I read the "Love is just around the corner" fortune I had no idea that the following Friday, right on schedule, he would enter stage left and leave my performance forever changed.

9

I like that I am unable to glimpse the future and know that a life-altering event is about to occur before it actually happens. If I were aware that something big loomed on the horizon, it might alter my behavior during the situation and therefore change the course or outcome. I have always said I would change nothing in my life because I really want to know how this ole gal I call myself lives out the rest of her days, and besides, I really like life the way it is. Better that we are caught unawares and forced to fumble our way through life to the best of our ability, without being given a dress rehearsal.

So it goes, during a late afternoon in November 2004, I was preparing to drive from Boulder to Denver to catch up with one of my sister's classmates from law school. He was in Denver doing an internship and my sister suggested that we meet. I was preparing to leave Boulder for Denver and decided on a quick stop to get some cash from an ATM and feed my chai addiction. I drove to a shopping center in south Boulder where I could kill two birds with one stone. Little did I know I would be killing three birds. *Knock that husband right off of your to-do list, why don't you.*

After the ATM I proceeded to Café Sole to get that chai. I pulled into a parking space and got out of the car. Now I *could* tell you either of two versions of this story—the mundane or the fairytale. I believe it'd be prudent to tell you both.

When living the single life it is easy to stay thin. An inordinate amount of time is spent running, hiking, and doing yoga because it feels good, but it's also in preparation for meeting the man of my dreams. Once the man is met, I'd rather loll about in bed with him than go running or go to the gym. And since I've found that special someone with whom to go to my favorite restaurants several times a week, suddenly that favorite pair of soft brown cords that looked so good on me go into a box and into the garage, in silent hopes that I will one day wear them again. I am aware that this is a shallow thing to mention, but we all have our issues and I *do* happen to be a female who came of age in the U.S., the only country where billions are spent on diet pills while every year approximately fifteen million children die of hunger worldwide.

This is all to say that on that warmish November afternoon things were definitely going my way. I had my game on, so to speak. I *was* wearing those favorite brown cords, and I was feeling good. As I approached the door to Café Sole I noticed a man, a *beautiful* man. He was sitting at a table outside the coffee shop by the entrance with two other men in the warm sunshine of a late November afternoon. And he was smiling at me. It took me by surprise, but I managed to smile back. *Holy cow*, I thought to myself as I entered the coffee shop. His face was soft and his features bold. He had dark hair pulled back in a short ponytail. His eyes were huge and green, and if you were not careful, you could quite possibly find yourself drowning in them. You'd want to drown in them.

What almost took my breath away, however, was his smile. The warmth and beauty in that smile made my heart skip a beat. It was familiar and inviting. It was soft and gentle. It suggested an understated strength, a humble quietude. It conveyed a willingness, a curiosity, a knowing. There was something in that smile that cared beyond the surface reality of one stranger simply happening to find the eyes of another.

Once I had my chai in hand, I stepped into the restroom to look in the mirror to see what this man was seeing, to look into the eyes that had returned his smile. My brown eyes were still brown, and my long, curly hair was still, in fact, long and curly. I was content that everything looked okay outwardly, and with that I casually strolled out of the establishment with an air as calm and collected as a morning breeze. I turned my head slightly to the left as I exited, and to my absolute delight, he was smiling at me. With reckless abandon I waded into that ocean of green.

The outward calm hadn't entirely translated on the inside. I grew flustered and looked away. This is a nervous response I have when I'm attracted to someone. If I'm at a gathering or function and meet a man I find attractive, I find it very difficult to look at him, much less speak to him. It's a form of self-consciousness—an insecurity, if you will—that has developed to protect me from the member of the opposite sex discovering what's behind my transparency. I've never been the flirtatious type. I drove off, leaving that beautiful man sitting in the waning light of that November afternoon. As I drove away I called a friend on my cell phone.

"The most *beauuuutiful* man just smiled at me," I exclaimed when she answered.

"Go back and give him your phone number!" she insisted.

"Yeah," I said out loud. "*Yeah!*"

It took about a nanosecond for those words to sink in and I found myself doing an illegal about-ship in five o'clock traffic. I sailed back to Café Sole. This time I pulled into a parking space on the other side of the coffee shop so his back was toward me, and strategically next to a large SUV that obscured the view of me and my seafaring vessel. I climbed out of my car and using the tinted windows of the giant SUV as a shield I watched and calculated.

The situation was not as straightforward as it seemed when I was pulling the U-turn to carry me back to the scene of the encounter. Indeed I was feeling confident, but not confident enough to approach a table of three men I didn't know. Had this vision of immense grace and beauty been alone it would have been an easy exchange. I could have approached him and casually said, "Here's my number." But *three* of them?

As I ruminated, one of the men in the threesome stood up and began to walk toward me. I dove into my car for protection. It turned out that he was the owner of the SUV, the Super Useful Vehicle. As he got into his vehicle I started my car and backed out hurriedly, trying to leave unnoticed. As I drove away, I felt a strong, nagging feeling that I needed to return, that I could not leave this situation loose-ended. Thank God for intuition.

I returned a second time, hoping he would still be there. As I approached the coffee shop I could see that he was indeed still sitting outside at the table. I was feeling flustered and sensed my game waning with the light of the fading November afternoon. My gut told me to pull into a parking spot, but my body kept driving. As I pulled back into five o'clock Friday traffic, that nagging feeling came back, and I chastised myself for not having more courage. How difficult could this really be? I was experiencing an internal tug-of-war. To do, or not to do, that was the glaringly obvious question.

Knowing now what I did not know then, I could have waltzed up to the table, handed that man my phone number, and said, "Call me sometime." I could have even said, "What are you doing for the rest of your life?" Although hindsight is 20/20, foresight rarely comes conditioned with clarity. As mentioned earlier, thank goodness for a strong sense of intuition that speaks louder than my intellect. For the third time I pulled an about-ship and sailed back to Café Sole. Three is my favorite number, and the third time is a charm. I knew this would be my final journey back to Café Sole that evening. It was now or never.

Afternoon had descended into dusk and I was a little more comfortable pulling up this time. The only problem was that he was … *what? Gone?* It simply couldn't be! My heart sank. I was disappointed that I had not acted sooner. I hung my head in defeat and started my car. I then noticed a man who looked suspiciously similar to my knight in shining armor sitting at a table inside. I realized with absolute elation that it was him.

I wasn't going to waste any more time. I scribbled my name and number on a piece of paper and wrote, "If you ever want to have a cup of tea." I realized I was not going to muster up the courage to approach the table myself, so I began to search for an unsuspecting passerby who could perform the act for me. Eventually a woman a few years my junior walked by wearing a Laund-UR-Mutt shirt. She worked at the pet groomer next to the coffee shop. I approached her.

"Would you do me a huge favor?" I asked.

"Uhhhh, sure," said the woman who would unknowingly seal the destinies of two mere mortals.

"Will you take this piece of paper to *that* man sitting there?" I said, pointing at Dan. "But wait until I have time to get in my car and get out of here."

The last thing I remember as I backed out was this unsuspecting destiny dancer tapping Dan on the shoulder and his look of surprise as she handed him the piece of paper. The following day I did not get around to checking my voicemail until the afternoon. Lo and behold, there was a message from Dan. He'd actually called at eight thirty that morning. Why waste any time? Later he would tell me, "When a beautiful woman gives you her phone number, you don't wait around." Flattery gets you *everywhere*, darling. And I mean *everywhere*. When we finally spoke that evening he told me that he was driving home from his spiritual group. ChaCHING!! A beautiful man who just spent his entire Saturday at his spiritual group? Is the universe taking special orders today?

Then the disclaimer: "I've been married before and I have three children. I need to let you know that up front. Do you still want to meet for tea?" Silence. Now *that* I was not expecting. My jaw opened and nothing audible found any escape. A small amount of time passed—a slightly awkward silence for me—during which my mind attempted to wrap itself around those words.

"Do you still want to meet me?" he repeated.

Once the surprise began to settle, I still felt drawn to meet this man. Intellectually it didn't make any sense, for I'd never entertained the idea of dating a divorcee with children, much less three children under the age of seven. But my heart felt compelled to meet this mystery man face-to-face. I'd already taken a dip in that ocean of green. I needed to hear his voice while I looked into those eyes.

The following morning we met at the Bookend Café, my favorite coffee shop in downtown Boulder. The fall morning was cool, crisp, and breezy. The dappled sunlight dancing on the bricks of Pearl Street kept me occupied while I waited for him. When at last I saw him walking toward me, I was overcome with that warm, intense feeling of a hundred butterflies all fluttering in my chest at once. I stood as he approached the table where I was seated outside. He embraced me as you would an old friend. It felt natural, familiar. There was nothing awkward about giving this man I was only just meeting a warm embrace. We chatted over tea for a couple of hours until he had to go to his spiritual group. I could have spent hours with him.

What arose for me during that first meeting was a sincere fondness for this man. He had great energy; he was soft and humble, very sharp. His words and gestures were deliberate. He was detail-oriented. And he was, in fact, doing his inner work. He was a dream, inside and out.

Still, I wrestled with the fact that Dan had three children already, as I hadn't thought about taking that on. I am a child of divorced parents who each brought step-parents and step-siblings in and out of my life. Dan didn't want more kids, whereas I thought I might. If you'd told me there was a great guy you wanted me to meet who was divorced with three children, I would have said no. If Dan and

I had each been on an Internet dating site, we wouldn't have met because he would have been in the divorcée-with-kids group and I wouldn't have had that box checked. Yet I've learned over the years to pay more attention to what my heart and my gut tell me than to heed the advice of my sometimes overly analytical thinking mind. Thank goodness when the universe handed me an incredible gift on a silver platter, I didn't push it away without another thought because it appeared differently from that which I thought I wanted.

Although I continued to have doubts occasionally, I let my heart be my guide. Most major decisions I've made have been from the place of what feels good to me, what resonates with my soul, where I am driven from the inside, not from the intellectual place of what I *think* would be good for me. Up front, I did not think I wanted to date a man who already had children. As I grew to know Dan, however, and things kept flowing with ease, I fell in love with him— madly in love with him. That which at first seemed impossible became easy and natural.

We spent hours in my little three-room cottage, curled on the couch facing one another, drinking endless cups of hot tea and sharing more dark chocolate than is prudent for two to consume. We grew to know each other over a few months without even kissing. Dan listened intently to whatever I had to say. He looked into my eyes, his gaze never faltering. He began to feel like that pair of soft, worn, ages-old cotton sweatpants that you wear all the time around the house and can never bare to throw away despite the hole in the crotch.

It's not that we didn't hit *any* roadblocks. I was flowing with that intuition, letting myself be pulled by that which felt blissful, felt easy, felt true. Then one day at work, several months into our relationship, a very wise woman who is all about "knowing" in the intuitive/spiritual sense said something to me about an entirely different situation that made me pause. "You know, Molly, you need to know who is floating down the river with you." Something about her statement hit home. I resonated immensely with the truth of it. To me it meant that I needed to know not only who I was and where I was headed, but who was headed there with me. If they weren't really headed there with me, I needed to get them off of my raft, because chances are they would only weigh it down. "Open your hand and let the dead wood drop," says that wise Zen master.

Dan was clear that he did not want more children. I was on the fence. It'd been a topic we discussed maybe once or twice but hadn't resolved. By this point I was madly in love with him.

We were nestled on my couch after work listening to David Grey, which is kind of solemn music anyway, when I decided to open Pandora's box. I could feel the anxiety in a ball in my chest working its way into my throat.

"Dan?"

"Yes, Molly?"

"I need to speak to you about something."

He sat in silence for a long moment. "Okay."

"Listen, I really think we should talk about the kid situation—you not wanting any more, me maybe wanting them. I feel like I need some clarification. Are we being honest with ourselves? I'm in love with you and I need to know where we stand."

"I don't know what to say." An excruciatingly long silence ensued. Then he got up, slowly collected his things, and left me there on the couch. My heart sank. My eyes filled with tears. He walked toward the door and on his way he picked up his slippers. They'd made a permanent home in my cottage since we started spending so much time together. He took them and left, closing the door gently behind him. I listened to his footsteps recede into the dark alley behind my cottage. I spent the snot-and-tear-filled night in a fetal position.

The next morning I found the following letter on the windshield of my car:

Sweet girl,

By now, you and I have talked, so you know much of what I am about to write but as you know, expressing my feelings is very hard for me. So, in addition to talking with you, I thought I would also write you this note.

Sharing my life with you over the last months has been out of this world. It has also been the greatest time of my life. You have shown me an unconditional love that I have never experienced. You and I have shared ourselves at levels that I have only dreamed of. In the last week I have projected us living long, healthy, and happy lives together sharing all of the ups and downs along the way. I've seen us traveling to the ends of the earth together and back again. I've seen us exploring the depths of our souls together. I've even seen your eyes as one of us takes our last breath in this world. I've also seen so much more.

As you can tell, I too am in love with you. You are an amazing, beautiful, and sensual being with so much love to give. In addition to giving, you are also learning to receive. You have opened your heart to me more and more and let me love you. For me, loving you has been so easy and warm and comfortable, and you have done nothing but reciprocate that love. When I'm with you, I don't want to be anywhere else. Could it get any better?

The connection I feel with you transcends normal levels. As you started talking last night, I knew what you were going to say and I felt paralyzed. My stomach felt sick, my heart was so heavy, and my mind raced uncontrollably, repeating a variety of statements centered around the theme that "it was too good to be true." As I stilled my mind, I realized that we must let go, but I just couldn't do it at

*that time. I knew you were prepared for that, but I really
wanted to sit with your words and make sure it was our
only option.*

*After sitting with it for the last twelve hours, I know that
I cannot go down the path you have chosen and therefore,
I must say goodbye, sweet girl. I love you more than you
know and I hope your chosen path is everything and more.*

Love, Dan

The following day I was lifeless because my broken heart
chained itself tightly around my neck. I couldn't eat so I went to the
neighborhood grocer and bought a pack of American Spirit cigarettes. I spent much of the morning chain-smoking over many cups
of black tea, sitting outside on the little stoop behind my cottage. It
was February and the sky was cold and gray. Eventually I decided
I'd better reach out to someone before drifting off into oblivion,
never to return. I called my friend Celeste, and as we were chatting,
me crying, I heard a soft knock-knock-knock on my door. I didn't
really want to answer it because my eyes were puffy and I stank like
cigarettes, but I decided to see who was there. I opened the door
and there he was, big, sad, green eyes gazing back at me.

"I don't really know what I'm doing here. I couldn't get any
work done. I just can't stop thinking about you. Molly, I don't want
to be without you."

We were married nineteen months later. The kid issue—me maybe
wanting them and Dan not wanting any more—worked itself out. I
trusted my intuition with Dan. And I am eternally grateful I did. "Let
yourself be silently drawn by the stronger pull of that which you
really love," said Rumi. The only thing we have to guide us on this
wild, crazy ride that we call life is our intuition. What our heart, our
gut, tells us. When we let our heart inform our decisions, life flows.

Now the fairytale version of Dan's and my meeting:

And there came a time when the moon was high and the stars were aligned just so. It was not yet night so the brilliance in this celestial pattern was unseen by human eyes. The magnificence woven by an Unseen hand simply was, and it was in the heavens, and it abound. The wind was still and there was a slight chill in the air, the chill of the season descending upon the land. The land was tired and ready to sleep, therefore thankful for the brilliance above it and for the coming winter. In winter it seems all things may rest.

The story was not the same, however, for the creatures of this place, two creatures in particular. Their mundane tasks are not worth mentioning for it is the soul, the spirit, the longing that is the substance of this story. And so it came to pass that at the week's end she went about her business as she always did. Her intention, however, drove her to a fateful meeting. Because she was clear in her heart and knew her heart's desire, when the moon was high and the stars were aligned just so, the angels descended and fate had its way.

As she pondered the possibilities of this nightfall, an angel as beautiful as the rising sun kissed her cheek softly and whispered, "South, go south!" And she thought to herself, I must go south. And she did. And as her task in the South was finished, an angel as beautiful as the rising tide caressed her hair lightly and whispered, "Tea, go have tea!" And she thought to herself, I must have a cup of steaming tea for I am weary and I must go on. And so she traveled far and wide to the great House of Tea.

At this time, he, too, was weary with the day, the week, with what had come to pass. He, too, longed for that which is nameless, eternal. In that second when time stops and eternity travels forth, an angel as beautiful as his great green eyes laid her hand softly upon his heart and whispered, "Look up, simply look up!"

In that instant a movement caught his eye and his gaze found the upward journey, perhaps on its way to the heavens themselves. It is exactly then that his eyes found hers, and hers found his. He smiled a great warm smile into her eyes, the color of a fertile land. Their eyes locked and held for an instant a space where celestial music plays, a space where all things are possible, a space where judgment ceases and compassion grows into great tall trees. So it came to pass on this eve when the moon was high and the stars were aligned just so.

10

One of the many great things about Dan is that he is fully supportive of my pursuits. I wouldn't have married him had this not been the case. We each get one chance, one opportunity to dance upon this earth in this body, with this beautiful, wild, effulgent soul. It is our one invitation to express whatever it is that is dying to come out of us, whether that be a form of art or a need to see the world, to lay eyes on another people, to witness how they live, to experience the expression of the eternal in a distant land, or simply to be. I read on a T-shirt something to this effect: "Those who believe it cannot be done should get out of the way of those doing it." When Dan and I met, I let it be known that I intended to leave for a year to do some traveling. He told me he would wait for me.

I'd been dreaming of traveling to India for several years at that point. When people asked me why, I could have said it was because of the rich, diverse culture, the extremes, the food, the spices, and the mystery, but those were not the reasons. I longed to go to India for the same reason I moved out West when I was twenty-three, the same reason I became a nurse, and the same reason I married my husband. I was heeding a strong, internal pull. I was drawn to her. It's that strong internal pull that compels a person to pick up a paintbrush or a pen, that pulls someone toward the ocean or the mountains. It was not my decision. It was just happening.

Yet as I grew more bonded to Dan, the thought of being away from him for an entire year no longer sounded so enticing, so I scaled the trip back to several months. We decided to make the first month of the trip our honeymoon. We would travel through the south of India together and then I would continue on alone.

Unbeknownst to Dan and me at the time, we were married on

one of India's biggest holidays. Ganesh Chaturthi, or Ganesh Day, is the beginning of the festival that celebrates Lord Ganesh, one of Hinduism's most highly revered gods. Ganesh—the elephant God—is known to be the god of wisdom, prosperity, and good fortune. This festival is celebrated all over India. It usually falls between August 20 and September 15. That year it kicked off on September 2—our wedding day.

I married the man of my dreams, the life partner I'd been hoping for. I married the one who loves my lightness and my heaviness, the brilliance and the shadow, the clarity and the cobwebs. The one with whom I can simply be—without words to fill the sacred silence. I married the one who would say, "Sure, I'll go to India with you." The one who is exploring his inner landscape—the peaks, the valleys, the canyons—and all that flows within it. The one, I was to eventually find out, who could be with me as I suffered—truly suffered—and face me unwaveringly as I faced myself.

We exchanged our vows on a dock in Grand Lake, Colorado, surrounded by family and close friends, by massively rugged peaks, and by early September sunshine. The wildflowers still wore their stark colors brilliantly against the blue sky while hummingbirds sipped their nectar. The lake lapped the wooden pilings on the dock that held us. The green eyes that bore into my soul that day whispered the promise of eternity into the vibrations of every atom in my body. Together we'd written our vows. They were more of a declaration of why we were choosing each other than they were vows in the traditional sense:

Because you know my heart without my having to speak it.
I am humbled by you.
You are able to disappoint others to be true to yourself.
Your grace and beauty are profound.
You strive to willingly accept that which life presents.

You illuminate warmth, beauty, and light.
Above all else you embody the truth, the divine.
With you, I have found my home.

11

Three months after our wedding, our adventure in India began in Chennai. There is nothing you can do to prepare yourself for India. India is an assault on all of the senses. It doesn't matter how many wise travelers you speak to who have been there before you, how much good advice you receive ahead of time. Nothing can prepare you for India except for India.

Chennai is India's fourth largest city. It is located on the southeast coast of the subcontinent. We experienced her first in a cab on our way to Triplicane, an area of Chennai meant to be rife with other Western travelers. I surmised we might initially feel more comfortable if we blended in a bit.

It was warm and humid, and many foreign smells hung thick in the air. Wherever you go in India, there always seems to be smoke in the air, the smoke of meals being cooked on a fire, of cumin and coriander and curry and turmeric egesting from their earthen shells into a man-made creation, or of waste being burned—human, animal, or plastic. Then there are the perfumed scents of incense that waft from makeshift temples or ashrams—communities whose members work toward apotheosis. In a coastal city such as Chennai you also have the smell of seafood, of fish drying in the sun. All of these smells are India, and they are woven together effortlessly.

In addition to the smells are the sounds, the dominant one being the horn. In India horns are honked freely just to say, "I am here and I am trying to pass you," or "I *am* passing you," or "You pissed me off," or maybe just, "Everyone else is honking their horn so I'll honk mine for no apparent reason, too."

Then there is the traffic itself. It consists of people, cows, dogs, bicycles, bicycle rickshaws, auto rickshaws, cars, buses, and trucks moving effortlessly through what may appear to the untrained eye to be absolute chaos.

Eventually our cab came to a stop and we were dropped in the middle of that sea of life, of humanity, left to figure it out on our own. As we climbed out of the cab I scanned the periphery in front of our hotel, the Himalaya, and I didn't see Westerners anywhere.

After you have spent more than a few weeks in India, you begin to get used to the penetrating feeling of eyes boring into your soul. When I was new to her, dealing with a culture shock that hadn't even begun to settle in, this penetration seemed horrifying. Having people follow me down the street, hoping to sell me something, practice their English, or simply begging—time and time again—at first made me uneasy. I avoided eye contact because for a bleeding heart like myself, once the eye contact is made it's all over. Beggars are in survival mode so they don't easily give up, especially if they sense you're soft-hearted.

There is a disparity between the notion of personal space in India and personal space in the West. In the West personal space is real. It is tangible. It almost has visibly defined borders. In India it is nonexistent. In a country with over a billion inhabitants where it is not at all uncommon to have many people living under one roof, personal space is not a learned cultural norm. Coughing, burping, spitting, and farting are not exactly private affairs either. All that said, when you go to India your personal rules no longer apply. India attempts to undo a lifetime of doing in a few hours.

In the West we are far too polite to stare at one another, but in India it is commonplace and not considered rude. It is not uncommon to be stared at for five minutes or an hour, or have someone approach you to stare at what you are reading or carrying, or simply to check out your shoes. Initially, having that many eyes bore into my soul unleashed an unfamiliar discomfort inside of me. It forced me to look not only into the eyes of the other person, but into my own. Was it that I was uncomfortable in the faces of those who, materially speaking, had less? Was it a responsibility I felt, at a very deep level, with which I was completely out of touch? Was it an intimacy with the raw truth of suffering (the other person's and my own) that I had difficulty being with? Or was it simply that I began to feel transparent? After several weeks in India, my heart realized that those penetrating eyes boring into me were doing so out of curiosity. Indian people are not shy about their curiosity. They scrutinize, they touch, they initiate the action that might satiate this sense of curiosity—this need to know who you are, where you come from, what you look or feel like—without the slightest hesitation.

We checked into our mid-range accommodation to discover quickly the relativity of the subcontinent. What is "mid-range" in India would be far substandard to most accommodations back home. In India, if it has a sit-down flush toilet it is not considered a budget accommodation, never mind the state of the room surrounding the toilet. Our first night in India, the first night of our honeymoon, we decided to splurge. We reasoned there would be plenty of time to ease into a squat toilet later. There was no need to impress my husband because, after all, he was now my husband. So the tough-woman-who-can-handle-anything facade that I'd been upholding became as permeable as my newly purchased mosquito-net-made-for-one-tent that I pitched and crawled into, leaving Dan in the brown-walled room that buzzed with hunting mosquitoes. My mosquito-net-tent had a cover on the bottom so I didn't have to sleep *on* the mattress. You don't want to sleep directly on the mattress in India's mid-range or budget accommodation world.

Eventually we figured out how to use the squat toilet. I had no problem squatting over the hole and doing what had to be done, especially if the hole had those nice little tractioned foot-accommodators on either side so you wouldn't slip and wind up with one foot in the hole. India's elderly are undoubtedly kept fit by this style of doing one's business. Squatting is a heavenly posture for the knees, hips, and low back, and it keeps one's quads in relatively decent shape. What I never did figure out was how to use the little cup of water next to the squat toilet. I'm aware it is meant to clean yourself after you do your business—with your left hand, of course. I just never seemed to get it right. After repeated attempts at cleaning myself with a nice stream of water and only managing to soak my clothes, I eventually gave up, opting instead to carry toilet paper.

After checking into our mid-range Hotel Himalaya, we set out for our first walk in the city. Our goal was to get to the beach, but we just seemed to wander down one small side street after another, my husband's six-foot frame towering above everyone we passed. I remained focused on that frame of his like he was a beacon in the night. We thought we were oriented, but each small backstreet turned into another, and the people milling about, staring at us with their curiosity, had me flustered in no time. If the distance between Dan and myself turned into more than a foot or two, I'd yell at him to slow down, to wait for me. I didn't want to be any farther from him than an arm's reach. Finally we gave up trying to get to the beach and just wandered slowly down streets we happened upon.

Because the sides of the road were teeming with life—goods and wares being sold, cooking and washing, beautifully dirty children playing, laughing, shrieking—we were unable to use them and were thrust out into the streets of Chennai, left to dodge bicycles and rickshaws.

Dan and I decided quickly that we would try, at all costs, to avoid bigger cities. We were turned off by the magnitude of the noise and traffic. We wanted a slower rhythm. A steady stream of bodies moves along the sides of the street, seemingly dancing with the dogs and cows, though the cows like to have a lie-down in any inconvenient spot—inconvenient for the tourist just learning about this flow. There are bicycles meandering along an invisible path, yielding to the auto rickshaw, which yields to the taxi and automobile, which in turn gives way to the trucks and buses; all of this is accomplished with a honk, or two or three, of the eternal horn. The end result is a very loud fume- and trash-filled waltz. The degree of this chaos is determined by the hour of the day, the size of the city, and any number of other factors such as weather or festival time.

It does at first seem that there is no order, no method to the madness. What becomes apparent, however, is that there is a greater force working and that within the chaos is a flow. Is it the force of entropy? I was unable to sense this flow if I was afraid or had resistance to the chaos. If I stood on a street corner and waited my turn to cross, I'd stand there all day. The opportunity was unlikely to present itself.

To survive and make my way safely through the traffic to the other side, I had to do the dance along with all of the other moving entities—human, animal, and vehicle alike. This required me to simply let go of the fear and move into the flow, dancing steadily through open spaces, from one to the next, at times quickly, at times more slowly, until eventually the destination was reached. It required me to *have faith*, as Pop-Pop said to me in that dream. One must be alert and attentive but relaxed all at the same time. You can't think too much about it. You simply have to do it. Moving through traffic in India takes the same skill as moving through the seasons of this life.

This subtle understanding did not come solely with the first introduction to Indian traffic in Chennai. It did not come from riding on the back of a Moped in the rain at dusk dodging cows, bicycles, potholes, and buses, and totally surrendering in order to survive. It came from repeated introductions, repeated attempts at navigating, until the sinking in—the letting go—finally happened. After a month in India at my patient husband's side, the traffic became a practice.

12

The next stop in India was the small coastal town of Mamallapuram, thirty miles south of Chennai. We weren't quite ready to navigate the bus system, so we decided to take an auto rickshaw from Chennai. We discovered a group of smiling rickshaw drivers just up the road from the Hotel Himalaya. As a distraction from the flies and their chatter, we caused quite a stir when we approached them. The excited smiles revealed crimson betel nut–stained teeth. The commonly chewed betel nut, which produces a mild stimulant effect, comes from a palm. Those who chew the betel nut have a striking red smile.

Usually these rickshaw drivers operate like taxi drivers, every man for himself. But this was an organized group with a boss who did all the talking for them and arranged their fares. We agreed upon a fare with the *bosswallah* (note: *wallah* on the end of anything in India means one who does something, like the *chaiwallah* who sells chai and the *laundrywallah* who does the laundry). Our bags were faithfully secured into the back of the rickshaw. Once we got going, we realized that our driver spoke no English. He knew only that he was taking us to Mamallapuram.

There wasn't much we could do to help him when we broke down in the marshy countryside on the side of a major road headed south to Mamallapuram. I wasn't worried because in India the word *schedule* has no relevance. I was only hoping we would not still be sitting there at dusk when the malaria-laden mosquitoes came out to feast. They are out from dusk until dawn, and I had opted not to take the malaria pills recommended to me by the Infectious Disease Clinic back in Boulder. Most of the people I know who travel to the developing world and spend more than a couple of weeks there don't take all of the recommended precautions.

Those I know who have lived there take even fewer precautions. I opted for long sleeves and bug juice at dusk over the malaria pills.

Our driver made a lot of noise banging around the engine of the rickshaw, keeping us informed of his progress in Tamil. Every so often he would stop banging around the engine and with his beaming eyes and crimson-stained smile he'd climb in and try to start his chariot.

Eventually it screamed to life—puttering, spitting, and jumping—and we were on our way. He pointed out various places of interest, speaking in animated tones, and we smiled and nodded, though we understood none of what he said. When we arrived at our guesthouse in Mamallapuram and paid the driver the fair we had agreed upon with the *bosswallah*, he was clearly insulted. Thus began a cacophony of waving hand gestures and ranting in Tamil. The owner of the guesthouse came out to see what all the commotion was about, inadvertently drawing himself into the situation. When it was all said and done, the driver left, incensed and mumbling Tamil insults under his breath.

We checked into our small guesthouse by the sea. Our room was simple. A double bed draped with a mosquito net was the only furniture. The dark, cement-floored bathroom had a squat toilet and a shower that soaked the entire bathroom with each use. It was set in a green, leafy garden where Dan used the jump rope he'd brought for exercise. A chorus of foreign birds sang their revelry into life every morning before dawn. When the birds started at five o'clock, the Muslim music began from strategically placed speakers around town, calling all Muslims to their prayer mats. This went on for at least thirty minutes. Then it was the Hindus' turn. From the same speakers a series of ballads from the Vedas began. They sounded more like cheerful Bollywood songs than religious hymns. This was all happening as I sat for my morning meditation under the mosquito net. My awareness invariably drifted out of the window, carried by the religious cantabile and by gently swaying palm fronds that rustled just outside. I loved the feel of the morning from our little room, and I began to feel myself relax for the first time in the strange land.

We discovered a shop across the road from our guesthouse. Nestled into its storefront was a *chaiwallah* who undoubtedly made the best chai in Mamallapuram. We frequented the shop three or more times during the course of the day. There was always the morning chai. During this time we sat on a cement bench in front of the shop, welcoming warm rays of sun that drifted slowly off of the ocean on its vector to the west. We witnessed the town awaking from this vantage point: the cow with its massive curling horns sauntering down the middle of the street in search of an early morning respite from the heat certain to come; the schoolchildren in uniform, off for a day of learning; the dogs—the endless number of cachectic dogs—on a search for sustenance; the vendors on their way to the beach to wait for unsuspecting tourists. From this shop, Guna's shop, we began to know India.

Guna was a strong-looking woman who appeared to be in her mid-forties. What she lacked in height she made up for with breadth and solid presence. She wore her hair short like a man's, a wise move in the heat of southern India. She wore brightly colored saris, usually yellow or red. I noticed one morning that her face wore a yellow hue. It was turmeric, Guna informed me. It was auspicious to wear it. Turmeric has been used in India for well over four thousand years, dating back to the Vedic culture that used it in religious ceremonies. It is still used widely today in India—in cooking, medicinally, as a beauty product, and during Hindu ceremonies. It has finally started to gain reverence in the West due to its potent anti-inflammatory and anti-carcinogenic properties. It not only decreases the inflammation found in disorders ranging from rheumatoid arthritis to digestive ailments, it also inhibits the growth of certain tumors. I might consider wearing it all over my body.

Several times during the course of the day, Guna made an intricate design with a white powder on the street in front of her shop. She told us it was rice powder. It welcomed in the sun, the animals came to eat it, and it was good luck. This ancient form of art is called Kolam, which means "guise," and has been practiced by women in southern India for hundreds of years. It is done so that the family is blessed by deities—namely Lakshmi, the goddess of fortune and abundance. It was good enough for the holy cow that liked to have a lie-down on Guna's beautiful rice powder creation.

Guna was blessed with good fortune, and her shop was always busy. It was a strategic business move to have the expert *chaiwallah's* stand nestled into her storefront. Those coming for chai might need a pencil or an aspirin or a piece of cake or a bottle of water or a pack of smokes. The needs of man are many.

If a crowd of people waited in line for a chai, nothing about the *chaiwallah* wavered. His pace remained steady and the air about him calm. He, too, was solid, thick like Guna. His skin was dark. His thick bare feet were disproportionately large in comparison to the rest of his body. His brow wore a sweat from the humid heat of southern India and from the heat of his gas stove. His dark, piercing eyes did not falter as they gracefully danced about his workstation, eventually coming to peer into the eyes of his eager customer. The deep brown-stained strainer sent endless cups of chai into the bellies of men on their way to work, those wishing to sit and have a read of the paper, tourists, and children coming to fill a stainless steel pitcher for the busy housewife at home. Nothing about him grew flustered, and the constant hissing of his gas stove lulled one into semi-consciousness. His quiet, gentle confidence permeated the air around him. He illustrated that in this life, it is not what you do but how you do it. *Chop wood, carry water,* the wise ones say. And that delicious, steaming cup of chai cost less than a dime.

Mamallapuram is famous for its rock carvings that date back to A.D. 630 during the Pallava dynasty, and for its present-day sculptors who carry on the tradition of rock sculpting, chiseling away from dawn until dusk. It is one of the greatest concentrations of temple art in India, with fourteen cave temples, a host of sculptures, and a rather famous shore temple. Early travelers referred to Mamallapuram as the "Seven Pagodas," which some claim to mean that there were originally seven temples on the shore, six of which it is said have slipped into the sea. The existing temple is now a World Heritage Site.

We climbed about the rocky outcroppings on the west side of town, exploring the *mandapams*, pillared pavilions that guard temples, and the stone depictions of life in ancient India. Especially impressive was the massive hand-carved Shiva. In Hinduism, Shiva is the supreme god. He is always depicted as young and beautiful because of his command over death, rebirth, and immortality.

We encountered two security guards who were quite happy to practice their English and have their pictures taken. I felt slight alarm because they appeared so stern and official. Upon closer inspection, however, they looked more like two soldiers outfitted for a colonial war. When we began speaking to them, their eyes shone and their boyish smiles were brilliant.

We were almost assaulted by an Indian midget who wanted so fervently to sell us a solid ball of shiny polished stone carved with various tantric depictions of sexual positions, the likes of which I could never have conjured up. Those Pallavas really knew what they were doing. The heat must be some aphrodisiac. All I could utter when I laid eyes on that ball was, "Oh my." If he had been selling a small sketch of these graphic positions, I would certainly have purchased one, but who wants to carry a ball of solid rock through India? Lesson here: Don't sell rocks to backpackers.

Then we saw the monkeys. Among the exotic trees were families of monkeys resting in the midday heat, barely noticing we were alive. Come supper time the docile creatures became scavengers and roamed the streets of Mamallapuram like a street gang in Los Angeles' South Central. Even the mother monkeys foraged, their babies dangling rather precariously as they rocked back and forth from underneath their bellies.

As we walked through the thick, damp forest exploring the rock carvings, we noticed a young child, not more than ten years of age, who followed us at a distance. Every time we turned around, he would dart into the brush with the giggling flash of his smile trailing him. I wondered if it was simple curiosity or if there was something he was hoping to gain from an encounter with us. This went on for the better part of an hour. I caught a glimpse of his smile one last time as we exited the shaded, rocky park back onto the streets of Mamallapuram. We disappeared anonymously into the sea of tourists, and that gorgeous little boy vanished into the sea of Indian children playing on the grassy hillside.

We found a vegetarian restaurant—pronounced wej—that served a delicious *masala dosa*. That became one of my staples in India. It is a large fried crepe made from lentil flour that comes filled with a savory potato-onion-curry leaf creation. It is mouthwateringly delicious. It is much heavier than the *idly*—a steamed rice paddy served with *dhal* for dipping, if you are in the mood for a lighter breakfast. It's hard to eat *idly* when you have *masala dosa* as an option. The second meal of the day for me was usually the *sambha dhal*. *Dhal* is an Indian staple found in the north and south. It is made with assorted spices and various lentils, depending on the region. In the south it tends to be thinner and is called *sambha*. It became a staple for me along with the *saag paneer*. In the U.S. *saag* refers to spinach but in India it refers to leafy greens in general. *Paneer* is cheese. It has the consistency of well-cooked tofu. If it weren't for the dysentery, I think travelers to India would all return home ten pounds heavier instead of ten pounds lighter. Indian food is to live for.

It is said that fifty percent of travelers to India become ill with a gastrointestinal bug. It is also said that the first bout of diarrhea begins within three days of arrival to the Indian subcontinent. To avoid the fate of half of your fellow travelers, there are certain rules to follow. One, don't drink the water. Filter it yourself, or add to India's growing plastic crisis and buy bottled water. Two, don't eat a fruit or vegetable unless you peel it yourself. Three, stay away from meat. If the street vendor from whom you wish to buy that savory *samosa* has a yellow hue to the whites of his eyes, consider hitting the next one, as he probably has hepatitis. Common sense and caution go a long way.

We took our meals as an opportunity to get friendly with the waiters and learn a few words of the language. In India, eighteen languages are recognized by the constitution. In addition to those eighteen are more than sixteen hundred dialects and minor languages. In most places, English is widely spoken, but it is definitely appreciated when a foreigner attempts to learn some of the native tongue. Not to mention that the Indian with whom you are speaking gets a pretty big kick out of your attempt. The beaming smile you invariably receive in return is priceless.

In the state of Tamil Nadu where we began our journey, Tamil is the official language. Hello is *vanakkam*, pronounced wanna-come. Thank you is *nanri*, pronounced with a slight roll of the *r*. Please would be *tayavu seytu*, while goodbye is *poyittu varukiren*. A few words go a long way. One morning over breakfast our waiter thought a shirt would be a nice exchange for our little lesson in Tamil. His sister was getting married and he needed a shirt to wear to the wedding. He asked us to buy it for him.

His request was difficult for me. Indians know you have *some* money or you wouldn't be there, even if you are a nurse and not the CEO of a large corporation. Many are brave enough to ask for a handout. If I gave a little to everyone who wanted it, I wouldn't have anything left for my travels. I eventually listened to my heart. If I encountered a soul I felt deeply moved to help, I gave a little. Typically that was the person who would never ask for it.

13

We left Mamallapuram in a bus headed for Pondicherry. It was a local bus with excruciatingly hard seats and open-air windows. A Bollywood film was playing on a television mounted in the front of the bus as entertainment for weary travelers. Some buses have only audio capacity in which case you experience blaring Hindi music for your enjoyment. When you are lucky you get the whole caboodle, and we were lucky enough to experience Bollywood on our journey. Bollywood films tend to be centered on romance and are performed musical-style, with the male and female protagonists bantering back and forth in ballads of Hindi music as if their lives depended on it, surrounded by a singing and dancing entourage often clad in bright, brilliantly colored traditional dress.

As we made the journey south to Pondicherry, we rode through marshy tidal areas peppered with small villages constructed of straw-thatched huts. I caught a glimpse of everyday life in rural India—cutting wood, picking something edible from the bush, digging for clams, tending to the fishing nets, tending fires that were always lit. Older women sat together in a circle while half-naked children ran about them, the children's laughter carried into the wind. Life seemed refreshingly simple.

We arrived in Pondicherry, fondly known as Pondi, and found it much to our liking. It was a comfortable town. The tree-lined streets were old and perfect for strolling and taking in Pondi's French architectural heritage. The whitewashed buildings were splashed with vibrant orange and pink bougainvillea. The French settled Pondicherry in the early 1800s. Today it is known as the Union Territory of Pondicherry.

We strolled the beach road before sunrise, admiring those who had risen before dawn to venture out into the quiet, humid morning to do yoga by the sea, to sit and meditate with the rising sun, to listen to the waves quietly lap the shore, or to get their exercise by power walking in their *lungis*. There was something for everyone at that hour on the Bay of Bengal.

We found a breakfast nook on the ocean and sat down to order. We ordered sweet, black, milky tea as the sun peeked over the horizon. Its warm rays reached us as the Bay of Bengal rhythmically pounded the rocks with thunderous waves. I was suddenly overcome by an intense feeling of sadness. It swept over me like a tidal wave arising out of nowhere. Before I knew what was happening, I was sobbing—deep, reverberant cries that were unearthed and shaken out of me by forces well beyond my recognition. Whatever was arising was old, very old, and coming from a deep, deep place. A meditation teacher once told me that when you encounter frequencies that are vibrating at the same frequency as certain things inside of yourself, they are unearthed, loosened. Experiencing them as they surface can be less than pleasant. I sense that India's vibrations are so strong that she forces things up and out.

At first we stayed at the Surya Swastika guesthouse for the equivalent of $1.50 a night. Until our arrival in India, I was unaware that the swastika is a symbol that dates back thousands of years and stands for peace and good luck. The swastika appears on artifacts from ancient Troy dating back to 1000 B.C. and has since been used by many cultures, including those found in Europe, Japan, China, and India. It is still commonly used in Eastern religious traditions such as Hinduism and Jainism.

The Surya Swastika seemed like a good launching point for us in Pondicherry. A ten-minute walk from the beach road, it was in the budget range, a few steps below mid-range, which translated into a filthy squat toilet, brown walls to match the brown mattress, no window or ventilation whatsoever, with one wall not quite reaching the ceiling that forced us into our next-door neighbor's foray into smoking, that usually started just as we were settling in for the night. Better that the room was dark because I didn't want to know what was crawling around down there on the floor. One night I awoke to groans emanating from the bathroom. There was splattering and moaning and smoke wafting in from the room next door.

Earlier in the day we'd stopped to enjoy the raindrops of a late morning rain drip and stream from the tarp over a food stand on the side of Nehru Street. It was a bustling operation with Indians coming and going, ducking in for a respite from the rain, then continuing on, taking their breakfast with them wrapped in newspaper. The delicacy of the morning was something fried—a potato mixture—with a white sauce poured over the fried patties. If Dan had simply stuck to the fried patties he might have come away unscathed, but he was feeling adventurous and went for the whole shebang. Unbeknownst to him, microscopic one-celled organisms lurked in the white sauce—which undoubtedly contained water—just waiting to get into his gastrointestinal tract. Rule number one: *Don't drink the water*, even if it is hidden in that lovely velvety-looking sauce. By late after noon he had loudly rumbling intestines, and by the time I was rescued by slumber, his bowels really kicked in.

I was able to prove my love by cleaning up after him when he missed the squat toilet in the middle of the night. Picture this: My beautiful Dan—pale and sweating—with his underpants wrapped around his ankles, moaning in squat position, the scourge of the third world splattering out from underneath him. And there's me—a veritable Florence Nightingale—rushing to his rescue in an attempt to make some sense out of the biology experiment there on our bathroom floor. If you want to test the truth of your marriage vows, go immediately to India. Do not pass GO, do not collect $200, and for God's sake *do not drink the water.*

After that less-than-pleasant experience, we found other accommodations that had a proper sit-down toilet and a tile shower that I felt comfortable stepping into with my bare feet. It's too difficult to deal with a high fever, diarrhea, and a squat toilet at the same time. Dan is tough, but that is too much to ask of anyone.

The Park Guest House is run by the Sri Aurobindo Ashram and sits on the Bay of Bengal. It costs around $9 to $10 a night. I could have stayed there for weeks. Our room was spacious and airy, with large windows and a little balcony that overlooked the bay. The gardens were colorful and well kept, with palm trees lining the courtyard. There were small rock-scaped pools with vibrantly hued flowers dancing about their edges in flames of pink and orange. Before sunrise I made my way outside to the meditation room on the second floor of a separate building that opened right out onto the sea. I opened the windows and meditated while the sound of the waves and the warm breeze welcomed dawn. Once the sun rose, the little fishing boats dotted about the water's surface appeared, evidence that the lanterns dancing on the water before dawn weren't actually ghosts. On my way back to our room, my heart smiled at the people who quietly stretched their bodies in various *asanas*, or yoga postures, in the stillness of the morning there by the salt water. I silently wished them well on their journey into presence in the body.

In the center of the historic French district, we found a temple with an enormous live Ganesh standing sentinel outside. Ganesh is revered as the Remover of Obstacles and the Lord of Beginnings. This elephant's head was elaborately decorated with beautifully painted designs and an OM in the center of her massive forehead. *Om* is a sacred syllable within the Hindu, Jain, and Buddhist traditions. It is less a word and more of a philosophical sound. It is representative of the source of all-that-is manifest and unmanifest. It is supposedly the sound of the universe when it created itself.

From nothing to something—two sides of the same unbound, unbridled coin.

This elephant's intelligent yellow eyes scanned the crowd for those willing to hand over a few rupees. She was trained to take the coins from your hand and give you a bonk on the head with her enormous trunk in a form of blessing. It took a few visits before I found the courage to approach her with a coin. She was enormous and capable of squashing me with one errant movement of her tree trunk–sized leg. I clutched my rupees as fear and adrenaline surged through my body.

"Go on," Dan said, nudging me toward the enormous beast. "She won't bite you." I stood a moment more, watching men, women, and small children alike hand Ganesh their coins and bow to her after she bonked them on the head with her trunk. I took a deep breath, and with dogged determination I approached the animal. *The only way out of fear is through fear.* I held out my hand as I approached her. In what felt like slow motion, her prehistoric trunk came toward me, and before I knew it my coins disappeared into its dark depths. Next came a slimy bonk on the head. I touched my hand to my heart, thanking her for showing up and helping me move through some fear—Remover of Obstacles and Lord of New Beginnings.

We ventured there in the evening on more than a couple of occasions. After the day was done, one of the most pleasant pastimes I discovered in India was walking around with Dan in whatever town we happened to be in, experiencing and taking in life. On more than one occasion we witnessed a ceremony being held inside of our elephant friend Ganesh's temple. Ganesh was led into the temple followed by a sea of cacophonic revelers screeching their horns and banging their drums and dancing in a fervor of worship. The elephant didn't seem fazed by any of this.

How absolutely fantastic it would be to blow a horn and bang a drum and dance with the neighbors to give thanks to life, to the earth, for the abundance and blessings all around us. To shout out to the ends of eternity our gratitude for even a second of awareness of any of it. We were born to do this. That creative expression of gratitude, that revelry for life, is waiting to come out of us. I'm sure of it.

The beaches in town were not suitable for swimming because of the rock wall that lined the sea and the strong, swift currents. I was needing a swim in the ocean, as the heat of southern India is stifling at times. We attempted to get to the beaches north of town by a bicycle rickshaw driver. His eyes were bloodshot and he reeked of alcohol, but we didn't figure this out until we were in his rickshaw and at his mercy. When we were well on our way, we noticed his stashed bottle. Eventually we realized that he didn't have a clue where we wanted to go. We finally insisted that he stop and let us out. We had no intention of paying him because he was drunk, and his idea of beach and our idea of beach were not at all jiving. Another Tamil-ranting tirade ensued, and we walked away, insults rolling off of us like water off a duck's back.

We opted for a different adventure and rented a Moped. There was something incredibly exhilarating about riding around southern India on a Moped with my dreamy husband, the warm sunshine on my skin, long hair flying in the wind. I pressed my body close to his and witnessed life flying by me as we drove north to the beach. Sometimes I just like to say it in a whisper. *India ...*

At the beach we found a nice little stretch of sand away from other tourists. It was beyond hot and there weren't any palm trees for shade. I'd worn my bikini because I fully intended to swim in the great ocean. But I soon realized I was the only woman around clad in a bikini, and a group of older Indian men clad in *lungis* had gathered, stationed in a squatting row, to check out my action. To them, my bikini was the equivalent of walking around naked. It wasn't long before I put on Dan's extra shorts and T-shirt, and that is how I made my debut into the Bay of Bengal. Being a spectacle is one thing. Being a spectacle clad in a bikini perceived as naked is something entirely different.

After a few hot, sandy hours at the beach and a cold Coke under the shade of a palm tree, we visited a community called Auroville ("City of Dawn"), just north of Pondicherry. It is also run by the Sri Aurobindo Ashram. Auroville was founded in 1968 by Mirra Alfassa, known as "The Mother," a French woman who was Sri Aurobindo's spiritual counterpart and who was given spiritual authority when he passed away. Sri Aurobindo had a short political career before he began to explore things of a more spiritual nature. He was considered a yogi, a profound thinker, a man who achieved great spiritual heights. His main premise was that humans are "transitional beings" whose inner spirits are destined to evolve, in a spiritual sense, to superhumans, or as I like to think, enlightened beings.

Auroville was established as an international community living in peace and harmony with the goal of serving divine Consciousness, a shining example of what is possible when humans choose the inner journey and come together to serve the all-that-is. It is a community whose people work not for livelihood but to realize human unity. Originally intended to house fifty thousand people from all over the world, the population today is approximately twenty-four hundred.

We met a German fellow who lived there for five years and eventually left. He says Auroville doesn't work, that despite its good intentions there are still power struggles among its inhabitants, and that those who tend to have more money seem to have more influence in the community's goings-on. I think it is incredible that they are trying, however. I believe there is hope for us humans to achieve a level of existence that is more about unity and service, kindness and connection, and less about borders and special interests. What we all want at the most basic level is love. And this love is unconditional, universal, eternal, and what we are all made of. We arose from it.

14

We traveled next to the state of Karnataka on the southwest coast of the Indian subcontinent. While waiting in the small train depot in Pondicherry, our attention fell upon an Indian family. The father hurried and fluttered about as if Earth's orbit depended upon him. The two children, a boy and a girl, played with one another to pass the time. Their mother sat in graceful silence with her hands folded in her lap and wise eyes aware of her surroundings while keeping watch over their things. The children and their father wore clothes that were more Western in style than Indian. There were several traditionally dressed elders with them who I assumed correctly were the father's parents and extended family. When an Indian woman enters into an arranged marriage, she moves into the home of her husband and helps care for his parents. There are few better pastimes than people-watching in India.

Once we were all settled on the train, the father spotted us and made his way over to say hello, to practice his English, and to pick our brains. It turned out that he was an insurance salesman from the Indian state of Orissa and he'd decided to take his entire family on vacation while he did some business. His children's curiosity about the white Americans was eventually piqued, and they came over to join the conversation. Mostly they just smiled.

"Did you have a law marriage?" the father asked.

"A what?" I replied, not sure if we'd heard him correctly.

"A law marriage," he repeated.

"A *law* marriage?"

"Yes, a *law* marriage."

After a few moments we realized he meant *love* marriage, as opposed to arranged marriage. The *v*'s come out sounding more like *w*'s. We got quite a head wag from our Orissan friend when we finally understood his question. He was very surprised to learn that most Westerners have love marriages. We received an earful as he explained why arranged marriages are far more successful than love marriages.

"Arranged marriage not end in divorce like law marriage," he informed us.

His wife had joined us by then, so I was too polite to point out that the arranged marriage doesn't end in divorce as rampantly because the wife is essentially the husband's property; if she chose to leave her husband she would likely be shamed by her community and her family and would be unlikely to get custody of her children.

Once he learned that I was to be in India longer than my husband, he enlightened us both to the fact that I would have absolutely no trouble finding an Indian man. I am not sure why he felt the need to make this point readily clear to Dan. He then proceeded to explain that I would be far more attractive if I looked more Indian. He asked his wife to help me achieve this, and out came the thick black eyeliner that took the ensuing week to remove, the red powder at the juncture of my forehead and hairline to signify that I was married, and a red *bindi* just above the bridge of my nose, again, signaling that I was married. The adornment, accompanied by my deep teal *salwar kameez,* had me looking so Indian that later on the train ride I was asked by an Indian man if I was an Indian woman.

What I needed to do to complete my Indian look, according to the Orissan, was to invest in some bangles for my wrists and some nice silver anklets for both of my ankles. When I was sufficiently Indian he informed his wife that I was far more beautiful than she. His calm wife, who had eyes far wiser than he would ever realize, was no doubt used to such inane talk from her husband.

"I make the decisions," he informed us. "She supports them because she knows I am right," he said, head wagging and smiling all the while. *You have no idea,* I thought to myself.

I wandered to the end of our train car to escape. A few deep breaths and his voice faded into the warm air of the late Indian afternoon as it passed by. I stood at the open car door and listened to the click-click-click of the railroad ties. I inhaled the scent of grass, marsh, cows, salt water, smoke—life. I inhaled life. It was intoxicating.

We made it to the overnight train that would take us across the Indian peninsula from Tamil Nadu to the state of Karnataka on the Arabian Sea. We rode 2TAC, which means two tiered with air-conditioning. This is not first class but it is more than a few steps above cattle car. We had assigned berths with curtains that we closed for privacy. For sleeping I would take the top berth and Dan the bottom, but while we traveled along, reading and watching the countryside appear and recede from our little window, we sat comfortably on Dan's bottom berth that folded out into two seats. At train stations out in the middle of hot nowhere, vendors boarded the train and walked the aisle selling beverages.

"Chai, coffee, coffee, chai," they repeated in monotone voices that lolled me into drowsiness. I must have had half a dozen sweet cups of steaming chai and coffee on that leg of the journey. Although chai is the drink of the nation, southern India is also known for its rich, dark coffee.

I met an older Indian gentleman stretching his legs at the end of the train car, as I was doing the same. It turned out he'd attended the Colorado School of Mines in Golden years earlier. He and his wife lived in the U.S. for many years until recently when he suffered a stroke. His children in the U.S. were too busy with their careers to care for him so he and his wife eventually returned to India to be with their other children. He made the statement that "India is rich, Indians are poor." He said India was a wealthy country with vast amounts of natural resources, beauty, and intelligence but that the caste system was a disabling factor. A child born into this world, regardless of his will or potential, is deterred by this antiquated system. He also said that public education in India is a disaster. The wealthy send their children to the best private schools while the poor are left to fend for themselves.

As the light began to dim outside our window, we thought it wise to try and rest. We would arrive in Mangalore—our destination on the west coast—at four o'clock in the morning. I nestled myself into the top berth, trying not to touch the vinyl surface with my bare skin but rather stay in my little silk sleep sack. Just as I was growing sleepy, I began feeling feverish and achy. I tried to shake it off as too much sugared chai and coffee, but when the feeling grew more intense I became queasy. Eventually I had the urgency that far too many travelers to the developing world become familiar with. I scrambled from my top birth to the aisle and scurried like hell to the toilet. Only hours before I was gloating about the fact that I'd been in India for eleven days and had avoided the fate of half of my fellow travelers.

I was in the bathroom for most of the night. Thank God the train had a Western-style toilet in addition to the Indian squat toilet. The toilet on which I made my debut into the developing world that night was the likes of which you would never ever dream of sitting on back home with your bare bottom. There were precious few other options for me, however, and at one point as the world went black and I almost passed out, it was the filthy toilet that kept me from hitting the floor.

Our intuition is here to serve us, and far too often we dismiss it. Hours prior to the onset of this illness, Dan and I were eating at a restaurant and I said out loud to him, "I should not eat this." What was on the plate appeared benign, but in it was a bacteria that would alter my life. I had ordered a *papadam*—a crispy cracker-pancake made from lentil flour that is totally yummy—with chopped onions and tomatoes on top. One of the rules of the developing world is that if you're going to eat an uncooked fruit or vegetable, don't do so unless you peel it yourself. I'd strictly followed all of the good advice that would keep one healthy, and until then I had been fine. I didn't want to eat it but it seemed insulting to send it back. It is hard to waste anything in a country where so many are begging for food. So I disregarded that intuition and ate it anyway.

When we arrived in Mangalore it was difficult for me to stand upright, much less walk. We disembarked in the darkness of pre-dawn and I lay down on a concrete bench, rolling around on its cool surface to provide relief for my feverish body, and because it was no longer pleasant or comfortable to be in an upright position. I threw in a few miserable moans to be sure Dan knew how much discomfort I was experiencing.

"You're still better off than the guy with no legs down there," he said, nodding in the direction of a man with gnarled, bandaged hands, pushing himself along the pavement on his small wooden platform on wheels, moving slowly in the quiet, languid morning air. While he might've had a point, it wasn't helpful.

Our plan had been to head to the Summer Sands Beach Resort, a quiet beach retreat on the Arabian Sea just south of Mangalore. It was a shady beach retreat set amid swaying palm trees. With me needing a toilet every fifteen minutes, our plans changed. We checked into the Taj, a swank hotel with marble floors in the lobby, fine rooms, nice linens, and very clean bathrooms.

I was filled with relief to crawl into a yummy king-sized bed— the perfect combination of firm mattress with soft overlay and clean, starched white sheets that were heaven between my episodes of hell in the bathroom. By then I was purging intensely from both ends. As I endured that agony, Dan took the opportunity to lounge by the pool and eat French fries and pizza. His purging experience days earlier rendered him unable to stomach any more Indian food. He began referring to it as mush. During his down time from the pool, he joined me in bed to take a respite from the heat and humidity in the air-conditioning and surf Indian television channels.

Although I was unable to interact with him more than just moaning due to my compromised state, his presence was soothing. To awaken from feverish sleep and throw out an arm and have it come to rest in his lap beside me was beyond comforting. When you are brought down by something so violent and hellish, the sweet things about life become really sweet. I was carrying antibiotics with me, but I wanted to give my system a chance to fend the illness off for itself before I began taking them. Hindsight is 20/20. Lesson here: If you develop diarrhea, fever, and vomiting in a developing country, for goodness' sake help yourself out and take the antibiotics. Don't be that foolish Boulder chic who wants to let the body fight its own battle for a while. This is India, and the bacteria here are a completely different battalion than ours.

After two days of respite at the Taj, we decided to make our move to the Summer Sands Resort. My intestines seemed to take a time-out for a couple of hours in the morning, so we took the opportunity to make the thirty-minute rickshaw journey south. I was concerned that I might soil my travel duds en route, but at some point when traveling in India you really quit caring about such matters. Whatever happens *happens*. You deal with situations as they arise.

We made it to the Summer Sands Beach Resort intact. It was comfortable and clean—not really a resort by American standards. I prefer it that way. I am not the resort type. The Summer Sands had bungalow-style cottages nestled along a dirt road lined with palm trees, each yard painted with bright, exotic flowers of pink, orange, red, and yellow. There was a flush toilet and an above-average shower. This was important because my insides were still in agony. I was visiting the bathroom five times an hour.

My meditation practice stresses equanimity—observing what

arises internally without reacting to it. My threshold blazed new trails as I came to know intimately every stain on the bathroom wall, the breeze through the bathroom window where the little spider made his web, suffering to the point of wondering if I was going to shit the life right out of myself. In this situation you want not only a decent toilet but a decent shower. After so many hours on the toilet, eventually it becomes necessary to roll yourself onto the floor of the shower—there's *no* way you're able to stand at this point— and be bathed, be baptized, by a warm stream of water.

The fetal position became my modus operandi when I wasn't on the toilet or in the shower. Something profound takes place when you are thrust into the fetal position by forces well beyond your control. And when you surrender to it, there is a degree of redemption that occurs from being with yourself, unequivocally, while you suffer. From the big picture perspective, that is how we enter the world—alone. And that is how we will leave it. I suppose that any practice we can get along the way is really just continuing education. We should get credits for it.

During this soul-stretching time I developed an India-glass-half-empty attitude. I started to feel that India was more of a hazing than anything else, a hazing for some cryptic dimension that I might not be ready to handle. It felt like India wanted to know what my soul could withstand. I felt like I was being broken, as though I were a young green stallion that stepped into the ring kicking and bucking and was being asked to yield. All I could think about was that India was dirty, that there was trash *everywhere*, that people were hungry, that emaciated-looking dogs and cows roamed the streets rampantly, that it seemed so difficult to survive here. I grew almost averse to India during those days of drudgery.

In my Lonely Planet travel guide there is a little section dedicated to "when to seek medical attention." Well, I had surpassed the "diarrhea for forty-eight hours without abatement" rule, and I'd been spiking fevers as high as 103 degrees. When at last I noticed blood in my stools, it was time to go to the ER. We waited until late morning, the time during which my symptoms seemed to slow for a few hours, so I had a chance of successfully making the ride into Mangalore with clean britches. The guys at the reception desk called for an auto rickshaw and the universe delivered Baba.

Baba was proud in a subtle, suave kind of way. He was in his late twenties and quite a handsome fellow. Baba had soft, chiseled features, shiny, thick hair, and a tidy mustache. He was tall, with a perfect build, and wore loose white polyester pants with a light beige safari shirt. Something about him was so cool that being in his presence simply felt breezy. He moved with an air of nonchalance. The inside of his auto rickshaw was decorated with bold red and yellow flower leis, while the exterior was painted yellow with multiple works of art, not least of which were the black-and-white checkered side view mirrors or the flowing orange letters that spelled BABA across the front, so all who passed him would know who was coming. Baba's real name was Mayyadi, but I liked the way Baba rolled off of the tongue, breath-like. *Baaabaaahhhh*.

The speakers played his music so loudly that it reverberated inside my chest. No doubt he believed he was doing us a great service (and really he was), but the music was a bit much for my sickly state. To get from the Summer Sands to the center of town in Mangalore we had to drive across the Gurpur River. It was massive and blue and sparkled as the warm Indian heat blew in wildly from the sea beyond. We passed fish markets and in my frail, nauseous state the smell of seafood and trash became a repulsion almost too much to bear. We decided upon a hospital that our upscale hotel several days before had recommended. As we pulled up to the front gate, however, it appeared as though no one had been there in centuries. There was no way I was going in *there*. I was in urgent need of medical attention but not wishing to meet my end behind the brown-stained cement walls before me. When Baba saw my facial expression, in limited English he suggested we try Unity Hospital. He drove us to the front of the hospital, which was bustling with people—a good sign—and insisted he would wait for us no matter how long it took.

Unity Hospital was friendly and efficient. After I had been dozing for a few minutes on the gurney in the ER, an angelic woman in a billowing pink *salwar kameez* appeared from behind the curtain. In perfect English she began to ask me a series of questions, and it finally dawned on me that she was the doctor.

"Do you wish to be admitted?" she asked.

"No, thanks. I think I'll be fine after the IV fluids and the antibiotics," I said. After she left, the nurse came in and handed me a handful of pills.

"What are they?" I asked.

"Tablets."

"I know they are tablets, but what kind of tablets?"

"Tablets," I was told again. Back home I would never swallow a handful of nondescript white pills given to me by anyone. In India it's relative. I swallowed the pills.

The nurse came to my bedside to draw my blood. Afterward, she handed me a small glass vial the size of a large test tube.

"We need a sample," she stated matter-of-factly.

"A sample?"

"Yes, a sample," she repeated.

I was perplexed. I understood what kind of sample they were referring to, and I understood they wanted it in the little glass tube. But the tube was hardly larger than my pinky. In the U.S. we give patients a "hat," a large plastic container that fits between the toilet seat and the toilet bowl, and catches their excrement. Then the fortunate health care worker scoops a sample out of the hat with a wooden spoon and places it in a sample cup. This little tube did not come equipped with any of the aforementioned, and I had not exactly seen a supply of antibacterial soap in the ER's little bathroom. Needless to say, they didn't get their sample. I was not about to put my hand in the line of fire of what was coming out of me.

Dan was shuffled hither and yon to pay for the various services. To have my blood work completed, Dan had to go to the cashier with the doctor's orders and pay, and then once the samples were collected he had to physically carry them to the lab with the "paid" slip to have them completed. Eventually he had to go back for the results. It also went like this in the pharmacy. First he paid for the IV fluids and the medication, and then he went to the pharmacy to pick them up and eventually brought the goods back to the ER. We spent about three hours in that ER being well cared for by the doctors and nurses. We paid less than $20 for the visit, the blood work, the fluids, and the medications. When we finally walked outside, there was Baba, faithfully waiting to take us back to the Summer Sands.

15

Within twenty-four hours I was feeling better, and within forty-eight hours I was able to venture out to the pool and the beach without fear of soiling my duds. After that violent and intense purging, my senses were more astute. It was as if all of that purging had sanded me down further and my senses were refined that much more. That which was beautiful before became crisp and sensual. The pink, red, and purple hues of the flowers were more vivid. The sensation of the clear water in the pool bathing my skin as dancing streaks of sunlight played in the depth beneath me was beyond heavenly. I floated on my back in the cool water watching large birds of prey circle in the sky above me as palm fronds gently caressed each other in the late-morning breeze. I watched one pull apart a large rodent as it perched by the pool on a fence. The birds are called Brahmani kites and greatly resemble the eagle.

When I was finally able to venture into the Summer Sand's café for breakfast—until then I'd strictly been eating toast delivered to our bungalow—I was pleased to find porridge on the menu. I was disinclined to eat Indian food after my experience, so a cup of black tea and a bowl of porridge were absolutely delightful. We cherished our breakfast on the Arabian Sea, listening to the sound of David Sanborn's saxophone played over and over again on the loudspeaker. The Summer Sand's employees stood like sentinels, ready and eager to take our order, as several construction workers milled about out in the hot sun by the beach, the sea sparkling like champagne beyond. Eating became a meditation practice as I chewed my food slowly, cherishing every bite, happy for the sweet taste of sugar mixed with butter in my porridge. After being so sick for the better part of six days, I'd lost enough weight that my travel pants were baggy. Dysentery is *not* the weight loss plan of choice. Let me assure you that it is effective, but I wouldn't wish it on anyone.

While lounging on our bungalow's porch late one afternoon playing cards and listening to the call of exotic birds against the lap of the surf coming from the beach, we were approached by an elderly white-haired Indian gentleman. He walked slowly with a walking stick.

"Is it okay if I approach you?" he asked, not really appearing to care if it was or wasn't okay. I was wearing a white tank top and no bra, and felt a little shy about getting out of my chair to greet him. Things are different in India when it comes to the female body. He approached the porch and Dan stood up to greet him. I slumped into my chair further, not wanting to flash my nipples at him.

"I am Father Jos," he went on. "I used to be the priest at the local Catholic Church. Now I live on the property, just down the way there. I oversee the school and the grounds."

The coastal region of Karnataka had been heavily settled by the Portuguese, hence the strong Catholic influence in the area. It was going to be Christmas the following week, as evidenced by a larger-than-life-sized Jesus decoration that greeted us at the reception desk.

"I walk every night, about two miles. I meet my friends at the beach here and we watch the sun go down. Where are you from?"

"We are from the U.S.," Dan replied.

"You know, I met a nice German couple here recently. In the spirit of Christmas they donated 1,000 rupees." He looked at us eagerly, smiling, as if to say, "What is the American couple willing to give?" Silence.

"We'll make a donation," I finally said, more to end the awkward silence than out of wishing to donate to the Catholic Church. I reasoned to myself that it would help schoolchildren, regardless of their religious affiliation. More silence. Father Jos stood there smiling, expecting one of us to jump up and grab our money.

"We'll give it to you later," I offered.

"I live five driveways down. It's the one ~~. The school is there. I live in the house behind th~~ expecting you."

With that, Father Jos gave us a salute and continued on h~~ y~~ down the dirt lane toward the beach. We saw him walking on the beach on ensuing evenings, and he reminded us each time of the donation we were going to make "in the spirit of giving." It became so uncomfortable for Dan and me that one afternoon as we were lounging by the pool and saw him approaching (he hadn't yet seen us), we jumped up and ran around the side of the bathhouse, hiding from him. Then we became sleuths, only we were trying *not* to be discovered. I felt like a child who'd somehow been disobedient. It is true what they say about guilt and Catholicism.

~~~

Kanyakumari is the southernmost point of the Indian peninsula. It is also the meeting point of three oceans—the Bay of Bengal, the Arabian Sea, and the Indian Ocean. From its multicolored sand beaches you can watch the sun rise and then follow its arc to the west until it dips beyond the horizon on its way to Africa. Kashmir is India's northernmost territory. It is encompassed by three Himalayan mountain ranges from the northwest to the northeast. Between the trinity in the north and the trinity in the south is the vast expanse known as India.

As Dan and I bore witness to evening descending upon the land from the chairs on our porch, relishing the sweet succulence dripping down our chins from papayas we were eating with spoons, in revved a bike that had the look and feel of a Harley but was none other than a Royal Enfield. The bike pulled into the bungalow next to ours, and off climbed a young man wearing black jeans and a jacket, face obscured by a shiny black helmet, unaffected by the heat of southern India's late afternoon. The license plate on the bike said K TO K.

Roshan was a nineteen-year-old in the middle of his first year of university. He grew up in Bangalore and was meeting his family for a few days over the holidays before continuing on his journey. He'd decided to raise awareness for AIDS by riding a motorcycle from Kanyakumari to Kashmir. He had a press date that evening with a local TV station. Riding that distance in India was no small feat. The distance between Kashmir and Kanyakumari covers approximately twenty-five hundred miles, and we aren't talking nicely paved roads. I have heard it said that India's roads are potholes surrounded by some cement. Roshan was all spirit—think *Motorcycle Diaries* meets India. He was driven by something greater than himself to bring awareness and education about AIDS to the masses. AIDS is still an epidemic in India with an estimated two million people affected, predominantly in the south, where Roshan has his roots.

Needless to say his mother was quite concerned for his safety, but she gave him her blessings and he forged ahead. When we met him, he'd ridden from Kanyakumari, and all was going well. What was so unbelievable was that three months prior to his departure, our new young friend had never even driven a motorcycle. Gumption and courage. I guess it's all about gumption and courage.

He knew more about Hollywood than either Dan or I, and his knowledge of the U.S. in general was impressive. His curiosity and drive were inspirational. He even informed us that Brangelina was in Mumbai filming a movie. When Dan showed interest in his bike, next thing you know Dan was off and speeding around the Summer Sands Beach Resort on the Royal Enfield. When it was time for Roshan to go to the TV station later that evening, he knocked on our door so that we could wish him luck. This world is full of unsuspected heroes.

The next set of heroes was on bikes, but their bikes weren't motorized. And their heroism came not from some great act of service but from their gumption and courage alone. These were two British sisters, one a doctor and one a librarian, who were pedaling their Indian-bought-and-decorated bicycles around southern India together on holiday. They'd started in Mumbai and were headed south to Kanyakumari. They were fearless and so very cool.

When the day of reckoning was upon us, we followed Father Jos's directions from the Summer Sands just up the road to his little bungalow behind the Catholic school. His home was set back among banana trees and bougainvillea. With a collective deep breath we knocked softly on the door. Father Jos shuffled with his cane out onto the open-air veranda.

"Come in. Come in," he encouraged. He showed us to a couple of seats on the porch. We sat chatting for some time. He told us about his life as an orphan. Apparently, some Catholic missionaries helped him out along the way, putting him through school. He was forever indebted. Eventually the conversation turned to Dan and me.

"Have you come to India looking for spirituality?" he asked.

"No," I answered. "I have a spiritual practice. Dan also has a spiritual practice." "Mmmmm," he replied, with an air of disapproval, nodding gently to indicate he understood perfectly.

Eventually we got around to the topic of our donation. Dan handed him our 500 rupee donation, which was a little more than $10. In India this is an amount that most would be quite happy to receive. It was not, however, the 1,000 rupee donation that he had suggested when we first met. He looked at the money then looked back at us.

"A half a loaf is better than no loaf at all," he said. Then he repeated it again slowly, in the event we'd missed it the first time.

"A half a loaf is better than no loaf at all."

Is that, Father Half-loaf, what Jesus would have said?

16

We left the Summer Sands Beach Resort and boarded a bus bound for the Coorg region. This mountainous region in the state of Karnataka is rich with vibrant life. Our bus snaked its way up a road hardly wide enough for two passing vehicles, and the courageous bus driver somehow managed to pass slower vehicles while avoiding oncoming traffic. Miraculously we all survived.

As we made our way into the mountains, the banana and palm trees grew fewer and farther between and the air became pleasantly cooler. Flowering trees, coffee, tea, and spice plantations peppered the landscape. We struck up a conversation with a beautiful young Tibetan woman in her early twenties. She was attending law school in Mangalore and was heading home for the Christmas holiday. There is a large Tibetan settlement in the Coorg mountains, one of the largest outside Tibet. The young woman had spent her entire life there, never having been to Tibet. A special permit is required to go to the settlement, and the permit is very difficult to obtain. Our young Tibetan friend invited us to visit her at her home, declaring that we would not need a permit. As it turned out, there was a brouhaha in the settlement a few days prior to our arrival, and the Indian authorities claimed it was the work of "terrorists." Therefore, no tourists were allowed to visit. We never made it to the home of our gentle Tibetan friend.

During the bus journey, an elderly woman, a small boy, and a young man boarded the bus. The boy's belly was swollen and his brow was wet with fever. He lolled about in and out of consciousness on his grandmother's lap as she squatted on the floor of the bus, holding him while bracing herself against the rhythmical motion of the bus winding its way up the mountain. The young man stood behind her with a concerned furrow in his brow. It appeared they were in search of medical treatment for the boy, for I can find no other explanation why one would bring a small child so sick on a long bus journey. Back home that little boy would have been treated expediently in an ER. Here he would be lucky to receive medical care at all.

We stopped in a small village with an hour or so left in our journey. Big mistake to down all of my water and two cups of hot chai *before* boarding the bus. I never had to pee so badly in my entire life. Staying well hydrated in the heat is important, but you have to bear in mind that there may be no adequate toileting facilities. As we pulled out of the bus station in Mangalore, I already felt the urge to go. *This should be interesting*, I thought, aware that I was about to undergo a lesson in observing the discomfort that arises from within. For the first hour of the trip I was a trooper and remained equanimous with the increasingly painful sensation growing inside my bladder.

By the time we pulled up to the little village, I was saying *Lord Jesus* (pronounced Lawd Jesus) to myself, over and over. My mother is a born-again Christian from whom the "Lawd Jesus" originated, and in some situations I cannot find a more appropriate thing to utter aloud to the universe. Somehow I managed to get off the bus and gratefully followed my new Tibetan friend to the "bathhouse." To get to the bathhouse we had to walk into what appeared to be a small restaurant with dirt floors. We followed other passengers through the front room, climbed down several dirt steps through a second room full of long tables, men congregated around them eating, feet bare on the dirt floor. They were all sweating and everywhere large flies buzzed about. Eventually we made our way outside to the rear of the establishment and down a slope toward a small river. I spotted the outhouse where men and women alike were waiting. As I was beginning to do a dance and couldn't even muster a smile, my new Tibetan friend said I could go in front of her.

"Thank you," I said, and turned to enter the outhouse. An older Indian woman clad in a sari barreled past me, almost knocking me down, and made her way into the outhouse. I am decent enough to let an elderly woman go before me, but where's the courtesy? A similar experience had happened in the train station in Pondicherry. I'd been being totally disregarded and elbowed out of the way by Indian men until I was practically shoved right out of line at the ticket counter. Now, after finally making it into the roofless open-air outhouse, in the hot sun of a southern Indian afternoon with humanity's excrement shining beneath me, I had the longest, most satisfying pee of my life.

In the waning light of late afternoon on December 23, we arrived in Madikeri, a town of about thirty-three thousand people. We were aware that a Saturday night during Christmas would be a busy time, but we failed to anticipate that every room in every hotel and guesthouse in Madikeri would be full. We walked every square inch of that town looking for a room, but there were simply none to be found. We were beginning to keep our eyes peeled for a bench or a church or anything to call home for the night, though I was not comfortable with the prospect. We then heard a voice call out to us from behind a desk in a little shop. It turned out that this shop was a tourist office that doubled as a Coke and cigarette shop. The shop owner arranged treks for tourists in the region, and there was a little home in the neighboring village where his clients often spent the night. He assured us that we would be welcome to stay there for the night and have our meals cooked for a nominal fee. The thought of staying in a village home without electricity or running water was enticing to me—other than camping, it would be my first time experiencing life without those day-to-day amenities most Americans take for granted. He arranged the whole scenario, and we sped off in a rickshaw to the little village of Galibeedu.

We climbed a hill out of town on a narrow paved road and soon left Madikeri behind. We found ourselves immersed in a dense canopy of green, lush hillsides and rice fields. Eventually the rickshaw turned left from the paved road onto a rough dirt road and came to a stop. Our driver escorted us on foot along the dirt road, which was in the midst of a thick, tropical forest dotted here and there with coffee trees and cardamom plants. The dirt road descended into a steep hill and opened into an exquisitely verdant valley blanketed with rice paddies. There was a narrow path that wound through the rice field, climbing a lush hillside beyond where several tiny cottages were nestled.

Once we climbed the far hillside and arrived at the first cottage, the driver said goodbye. We were greeted by Savitha Rai, one of the warmest and most unassuming women I have ever met. The matriarch of the family, Savitha was twenty-eight years old and the mother of Harshita, wife of Prashth, and caretaker to her husband's parents with whom she lived. She stopped what she was doing to greet us and made us feel as though she had been expecting us for weeks. She welcomed us into her home and promptly had a hot coffee in our hands. Savitha's and Harshita's eyes were so gracious and loving, it felt like they wanted to imbibe our life experience, like they wanted to know us intimately. Is this how it is when folks live off of the land, day by day, unaffected by television and other technology?

Once our things were settled into the only room in the house with a bed, eight-year-old Harshita gave us a tour of the property. She spoke better English than anyone else in the family. Education is taken very seriously in southern India. Most of the female population is educated, though many women will still end up as housewives in arranged marriages.

The tour started in the kitchen, where Savitha, sitting on the dirt floor, had resumed her duties grinding rice in what looked like a large mortar and pestle. The rice, which came from the fields in front of the house, was for *idly*, our breakfast the following morning. No carbon footprint here. Then we toured the bathroom—a dirt-floored room with wooden walls, a bucket for washing, and a hole in the floor. Next we visited the cardamom-roasting hut out back where there were trays upon trays of sweet aromatic cardamoms roasting to be sold at the market in Madikeri. We were given proper introduction to the three pigs and five cows, all of which had names, and to the chickens that didn't have names. We also met Tony, the little dog tied to the side of the house.

Before dusk settled, Harshita brought out a little ball, quite possibly her only toy, and with a smile that was larger than life, she and Dan engaged in a game of catch. When Dan taught her how to catch the ball so that it did not fall from her hands, she erupted with joyous giggles. When dusk finally fell upon the forest, the rice fields, and the warm home we'd been fortunate to stumble upon, Prashth and his parents returned from a long day of work in the rice fields. We gathered around a kerosene lantern in the main room of the house to speak to one another in limited English while Savitha prepared our dinner and shadows danced about on the walls of the little cottage.

While we waited for our meal, Grandma summoned me into her room to show me the sari she would wear to a cousin's wedding the following day. She'd travel alone by bus to Mangalore to reach the festivities. The sari was bright blue with gold trim. No doubt she would be proud to wear it. She then proceeded to point to her feet and repeat the word *pain*. She'd learned I was a nurse and wanted to know what I could do for her pain. Given her age and the fact that she toiled day in and out in the rice fields, I thought it likely that she had a touch of arthritis. I pulled out my ibuprofen and gave her two tablets to take after her dinner. Then Savitha approached me with her complaints of neck pain. Watching how she sat on the floor bent over her large mortar and pestle, I gathered she had inflammation in her neck and gave her a couple of ibuprofen, too.

I did not sleep much that night. I was wide awake drinking in the place, the people, the culture so vastly different from my own. I arose during the night and went outside to take in the starlit sky. The silence was as deafening as the sky was brilliant. It looked like a million tiny diamonds shimmering their aliveness from light years away. The silence penetrated me. It became me. From that quiet mountain village in southern India, I could feel the universe breathing—the eternal inhale, exhale...

The next morning, both Savitha and her mother-in-law reported much relief from their pain after the ibuprofen, and thus they were given my entire bottle of ibuprofen with strict instructions to take only a couple of tablets twice a day after a meal. It was quite amazing to see something that I take for granted—pain relief—make such a difference in the lives of a couple of women who toiled much harder than I ever would.

As Dan and I sipped our steaming coffee harvested from the very land our eyes feasted upon that morning, I received a lesson in Kannada, the language spoken in much of Karnataka. Harshita, with her infectious smile and her young, wise eyes, was patient through all of my queries.

"What is *hello*?" I asked.

"*Namascara.*"

"*Goodbye?*"

"*Ogey bataney.*" At least that is how it sounds.

"Mmmmm, how about *thank you*?" I continued.

"*Vanda negalu,*" she said, smiling at me with her dreamy dark chocolate-colored eyes, long eyelashes fluttering as though she were a beautiful Disney character.

"What is *rain*?" I asked, scribbling the words in my journal.

"*Male.*"

"*Sun?*"

"*Surya.*"

"*Moon?*"

"*Chandra,*" she stated patiently, sidling closer to me to have a look inside of the journal in which I was recording her Kannada lesson.

"*Stars?*"

"*Nochatra.*" She gazed at me and I could feel her little body press into mine. The innocence and lightness that poured out of her was exquisite.

"How about *wind*?"

"*Gale,*" she said. "Wind is *gale*." (Pronounced gahleh.)

The village of Galibeedu was named after the wind that blows over its mountaintops and kisses the rice, the coffee, the tea, the cardamom, the vanilla, and all of the other spices that grow there. It was named after the wind that caresses the sweet souls who inhabit the land.

Sometime late morning Dan and I gathered our things and prepared to say goodbye to the family who'd touched us with their kindness, acceptance, and hospitality. At that point it was just Savitha and Harshita, as Prashth and his father had returned to the rice fields and Grandma was on her way to the wedding in Mangalore. Dan handed Savitha 1,000 rupees, which amounted to approximately $20 and would have been quite a considerable sum to her. She stared at us in disbelief.

"But why?" she asked, her sincere eyes looking back and forth at Dan and me.

Because your heart is as big as the rice fields upon which you dwell, because Harshita's school supplies are expensive, because that dear child deserves a toy or a sweet, because you need candles to light your kitchen at night, because you deserve something new and pretty more than anyone I know, because at home we would spend more than this going out for sushi and we wouldn't think twice about it.

"Because we want you to have it," Dan said.

As we strode across the rice field, we turned around frequently to return the waves of the beautiful mother and daughter. They did not stop waving until we were well into the forest.

Later that afternoon we were due to arrive at the Golden Mist, an organic plantation also nestled in the village of Galibeedu. We had some time to spare so we meandered about the streets of the village and I practiced my newly learned Kannada.

"Namascara!" I called out to the old man hanging out at the mom-and-pop Coke stand.

"Ogey bataney!" I said to the kids playing in the road as we strolled past them and continued on our way.

Eventually the heat got the better of us so we retreated to the shady bank of a small pond to read and watch the water bugs skate across its murky green surface. We were discovered by a family across the way, and it wasn't long before the man of the house approached us with his three children in tow behind him. I was alarmed by the scythe swinging back and forth from his hand as he made his way toward us. That is, until he broke out in a full smile. It was rice harvesting season, hence the scythe. The community works together during rice harvesting season. The Indian men leaning against his house across the road—their arms folded while they watched patiently with curiosity as the scene unfolded—were neighbors from Galibeedu.

He wanted to know from whence we came, where we were headed, and anything else we had to share. Within fifteen minutes we met the neighbors, who were then able to take the afternoon off, and were seated in his living room. The farmer's beautiful wife, lithe and shy, stopped her chores to make us tea and serve biscuits. We were the first white people to enter his home. It was a big deal to him. We heard about his running days—apparently, he'd been quite an athlete. His prized possession, second to a trophy placed in reverence atop his television, *was* his television. He assumed we would want to watch it with him, so he turned it on full blast and we shouted at each other over tea, biscuits, and Bollywood. Although this place was less than a mile away from our humble little accommodation the night before, where electricity hadn't yet found its way, it was quite a change. As the shadows grew long and the afternoon wore on, we said our goodbyes, making promises to return that we would not keep.

We eventually found the dirt drive to the Golden Mist Plantation. As we turned off the road, we found ourselves trodding through dappled sunshine and more thick forest peppered with coffee trees and cardamom plants. Large spider webs spun carefully under giant green leaves hid enormous, furry spiders. Bird calls the likes of which we'd never heard sounded out through the damp stillness. The moist earth was rich with unfamiliar smells. We discovered one of the most massive trees either of us had ever seen. We were so taken with it that we circled her circumference in awe, touching and smelling her, and eventually took refuge among her enormous roots. With our backs propped against the gigantic gnarled roots and our legs spread out before us, we gazed into the canopy at her massive branches, listening to the whisper of the breeze in the leaves and the back-and-forth call of the mysterious birds. The tree, called a champac (*Michelia champaca*), is in the magnolia family. This ancient tree with its enormous twisting roots was somewhere in the neighborhood of a thousand years old. We later learned that having one of these trees on your property is very auspicious. Her flowers are used to decorate idols and temples during *pujas*—acts of reverence or worship to the divine. She certainly blessed us during the remainder of our stay in the Coorg region.

The main house was perched in a clearing, surrounded by banana trees and a well-tended garden. Ludwig the eccentric German proprietor lived there. A second smaller home was nestled farther along a dirt path and occupied by Vasu, Vasu's wife, their teenage son, and two teenage daughters. Vasu oversaw the daily operations of the plantation along with its workers. His wife and daughters tended to the plantation guests, cooking meals and serving tea. Neither Vasu nor Ludwig could operate independently of one another. Their symbiotic relationship made this organic, fair-trade operation function. For guests there was a loft-style apartment attached to the rear of Ludwig's house. It had windows that opened out into the rainforest. There was also a plantation-style cottage tucked a little further back in the forest on the other side of ripe Arabica coffee trees.

Ludwig reminded me of a cross between my father, Albert Einstein, and a 1960s rock star. My father loves life and people and will go anywhere and talk to anyone. He knows something about everything. He is usually found running around because his plate is entirely too full—this as a result of his zest for life, his corresponding lack of discipline not to take on anything else, and a sometimes sparse attention to detail.

Ludwig the German also loved life and people and philosophizing, especially over whatever it was that he was always rolling with his tobacco. Ludwig had a passion for music, which he played loudly. His hair was light brown, not white like my father's hair, but had the wildish appearance of Albert Einstein's head of hair. The 1960s rock star resemblance had a lot to do with the disheveled look and his endearing "*Fuck,* man," said in his raspy voice that made Ludwig Ludwig. He also looked incredibly cool riding off on his Royal Enfield in his worn black leather jacket. He was always going somewhere to meet someone.

Vasu was a small man but his presence emanated from every cell in his body. He was quick and lithe, and his dark eyes could softly pierce the most hardened soul. While busily tending the plantation and the workers and taking care of the guests and his own family, he'd stop and put his attention upon you as if you were the only person in the world who mattered to him. He said little, but when he spoke you listened.

That afternoon, Vasu gave us a tour of the plantation. We sauntered among the coffee trees learning the difference between Arabica and Robusta coffee. Both are grown on the plantation under the shade of the rainforest. Arabica coffee, considered by most the finer coffee, takes longer to grow and is more fickle about its environment than the Robusta coffee, which is typically used as supermarket-grade coffee. We toured the tea plants, the rice fields, and the spices—the cardamom, vanilla, and other spice plants that grow readily in the humid, lush environment. This small fair-trade plantation did everything by hand. Nothing was mechanized. The coffee was picked by hand, the tea by hand, and the rice entirely by hand.

There were dark-skinned workers with brightly colored clothes, feet bare, scythes swinging back and forth harvesting the rice crop. After cutting the crop, they brought it to a central holding area where it would be pounded into the ground so that the rice grain was expelled. The Golden Mist Plantation shipped its tea, coffee, and rice to a few specialty shops in Goa and in Germany. The workers who came from Galibeedu were from the lowest class of the caste system. Ludwig paid them well and took care of their medical needs and their families. In return, they were loyal and hardworking.

Our first several nights on the plantation we stayed in the apartment attached to the rear of Ludwig's house. In the mornings, Vasu or one of his daughters arrived with tea or coffee and a scrumptious Indian breakfast. We ate this in front of our open windows listening to the rainforest awaken, bird call by bird call. By lunch on our second day we were eating most of our meals with Ludwig in his living room. By day five we were sleeping in the loft above his living room because there were more plantation guests than rooms. Dan was in seventh heaven because he was sick of Indian food and

Ludwig had hearty bread, salami, and mustard. We had a mutual affinity for one another. After supper in the evenings we lit a fire in an outdoor fireplace, and the other plantation guests joined us there. We sat in chairs close to the fire watching sparks twirl into the night sky overhead, listening to the pop and crack of the fire. We spoke of everything from India to George Dubya Bush to cooking school in Italy while Ludwig's rock 'n' roll music blared from an open window in the house.

We spent our Christmas holiday nestled around the fire under the canopy of the rainforest with Vasu and Ludwig. There was a poinsettia growing out of the earth just above the fire pit. Vasu's son arrived with a very special Indian Christmas dinner—special because it was Dan's and my first Christmas as husband and wife and we were out in the world alone together, and because of the effort that Ludwig, Vasu, and his family were making to give us a Christmas holiday—complete with his version of the menorah. Apparently, a Jewish man who stayed there recently created a menorah for himself, so on a block of wood Vasu's son melted seven candles and delivered them to us with pride. We ate by those seven dancing flames and listened to the sounds of the night—tree frogs, crickets, small animals moving in the darkness, the distant sound of drums—come alive on the sultry December evening. My being felt part of an energetic equilibrium in exchange with the all-that-is, ever-was, or will-be.

~

The morning after Christmas, Vasu and his two daughters woke us just before dawn. We silently walked with them as the day broke, listening to the birds wake up in the canopy that surrounded us. Vasu led us through rice fields and into a forest that turned into a valley settled with fog. We made our way to the highest mountain in the region. When we began to climb, we found ourselves floating above the fog. Vasu provided a lesson in the local flora and its uses. He was thoroughly impressed that Dan and I were able to keep up. Evidently, we were the first tourists he'd ever taken on that hike who were able to keep his pace. Must be the Colorado in us. When we reached the summit, Vasu pulled several hard-boiled eggs from his coat pocket as our treat for reaching the top. The smile that spanned his face from ear to ear was worth a thousand priceless words. We ate our eggs in silence and braced ourselves against the fierce *gale*.

The following day we journeyed to a neighboring organic plantation called the Rainforest Retreat. The owners were an Indian couple who married a little later in life in a love marriage after both had earned their Ph.Ds. They'd been researchers in Delhi and eventually left their research jobs to start their organic plantation. They founded WAPRED (Worldwide Association of Preservation and Restoration of Ecological Diversity) to raise awareness of the toxic pesticides and fertilizers destroying the fragile, biodiverse ecosystem there and elsewhere. Graduate students from universities in India performed research on their property to learn, for example, which insect or worm could be introduced to eat the weeds but leave the crop alone; which herb could be sprayed as a weed deterrent but would not affect the crop; and which plant could be sowed around the crop so the insects would eat *it* and leave the crop alone. Apparently, fermented cow urine is an effective pesticide. Using it on the plantation eliminated the need for harmful chemicals.

Dan went on motorcycle rides with Ludwig while I played in the dirt weeding the garden, happy to inspect different species of butterflies and frogs. Ludwig helped me get over an insecurity about being an American traveling abroad. When we set out for India, I was embarrassed to admit to people that I was from the country whose then administration cared more about oil than international relations, its own population's health, the natural environment, or humanity in general. I felt like I needed a T-shirt that said I DIDN'T VOTE FOR DUBYA. I found acceptance, understanding, and a perspective shift at the Golden Mist Plantation.

We do not interact with nations—we interact with people, with other human beings. Ludwig could relate to my feelings since he is a German. He said he felt similarly when he first started traveling, as he came from the country where Hitler hadn't been kind. The truth of the matter is that people are people and the human spirit is unconditional. We may take humanity and put it neatly into bits by calling this person German and that person Indian or American, but the essence of what we are can't be put into bits. We all share the same fears and desires. We all arise from the same vast, eternal place, and we will all return there one day. Truth is, we never left that place. When we judge another we are actually judging ourselves. After our time with Ludwig, my perspective of my country shifted. The U.S. is a nation settled by brave and courageous men and women seeking justice and freedom. I'm still part of that.

Two days before we left the Golden Mist Plantation, my dysentery returned and with it a wicked bilateral pink eye. When I woke in the morning my eyes were glued shut. They were as pink as some of the lovely flowers on the property. I assumed the infection resulted from dirt getting into my eyes on the bus ride from Mangalore to Madikeri a week earlier. We visited the same ER in Mangalore a second time for some antibiotics, for both my gut and eyes. I should have been clued in when the doctor told me he wanted to admit me to keep an eye on me for a day or two. I declined because we'd already purchased train tickets and our train was departing that evening—New Year's Eve—for Chennai. Furthermore, Dan's flight back to the U.S. departed from Chennai the following night.

Guna's shop (me and cow perched in front), *chaiwallah* to the right serving chai to a child

Dan, Mamallapuram

Security officers or soldiers, Mamallapuram

Street toughs

High-rent district,
Pondicherry

Sunrise from the
Park Guest House,
our sanctuary in
Pondicherry

Sizing up Ganesh,
Pondicherry

Getting closer to
Ganesh in the light
of day

The Orissan's wife
and me

Summer Sands Beach Resort, Mangalore

Dan and Baba

Me and Father Jos

Roshan—gumption and courage

Sexy

British sisters and their chariots, Summer Sand Beach Resort

Savitha grinding rice
for *idly*, Galibeedu

Grandma and
Harshita, Galibeedu

Ludvig, Vasu, and his daughters, me and Dan, Galibeedu

Harvesting rice by hand, the Golden Mist Plantation

'Tis the season. Dan, me, and Vasu—Golden Mist Plantation

On top of the world. Day-after-Christmas hike with Vasu and his daughters

Michelia champaca tree, to which no photo could possibly do justice

part three

This place where you are right now,
God circled on a map for you.

—Hafiz

18

I've survived nearly a week at Breach Candy Hospital by myself. I've actually gotten into a rhythm. Teatime happens three times during the day, which makes the entire experience bearable. A cup of black tea, my all-time fave, with biscuits makes hell a much nicer place to be. My sister calls after breakfast, which is just before my sponge bath. Then the doctors make their rounds. I have free time to doze or write in my journal from about eleven o'clock until lunch. The darkness that overcomes me during the long night is shed with the sun, and my hopeful, positive attitude endures well into the morning. After lunch there is more rest time. Four o'clock is teatime. During or just after tea, my mom calls. Then it's time for physical therapy and finally, supper. As shadows grow long and the night looms ahead, the pain grows worse and the anxiety and fear emerge. The night then stretches out before me. It awaits, filled with darkness—my darkness; fear spirals out of me from places yet unseen by my eyes, places not traveled by my conscious mind.

After dinner I usually get phone calls from my brother, my father, or one of my close friends. It is starting to feel like I spend most of my time on the telephone. This seems about right because normally in a situation like this—having found yourself incapacitated and in the hospital—you'd be surrounded by loved ones. I don't have any visitors except for Christy from the embassy who has stopped by a couple of times.

I am just finishing my sponge bath. It's been almost a week since I washed my hair. Back at Boulder Community Hospital a sweet little nursing assistant created an acronym for this type of bathing —PTA. That's Pits, Tits, and Ass. The essentials. That won't mean anything to you unless you've spent time in the backcountry, spent more than a few days in the hospital, or you have a loved one who has. Bottom line: You can only wash your PTA so many times without a real shower before you start to stink. Maybe the doctors and nurses don't smell me, but I smell myself. I *really* need to wash my hair.

Ardi and another nurse are changing my sheets, and I've just managed to get my pajamas on. As Ardi puts the clean sheet under me, I use the walker placed strategically next to the bed to get myself to a standing position. Ardi and I work well together. There is a knock-knock-knock at the door. She rushes over to man the door, as we are still in bath mode and it wouldn't be appropriate for a male doctor to enter and see me half-dressed. I hear a female voice on the other side. Ardi opens the door just a crack to see who it is.

In walks my friend Ashley, three feet of extra girth strapped to her back with the enormous pack she is carrying. As soon as our eyes meet, I burst into tears. She manages to shove her pack in a corner of the room before embracing me tightly with both arms. The floodgates open wide. Tears turn into sobs with the immense relief that comes from feeling I am no longer floating out on the wild sea alone. The familiarity of having someone in my presence who *knows* me after so many days of being a stranger to everyone, of being the American patient in room 325 whose husband, the doctors have decided, has left her stranded in India, is more than a relief.

Ashley is a wild, young thing. She and I began working together at Boulder Community Hospital circa 2003. We took a liking to one another immediately. Eventually we began sharing our mutual dream to travel. I was already planning the India trip, and it didn't take much to convince her to hit the road, too. She'd been thinking about it for a while and just needed to be galvanized. At the age of twenty-four she had the gumption and courage to make it happen. We made plans to meet up in India. Of course, it wasn't supposed to happen like this.

By the time Ashley got to me in Mumbai, she'd been traveling for three months. She started her travels in Thailand, trekked around Bhutan, and then went on to Nepal. She'd been making her way down through northern India when she received the desperate e-mail from my mother letting all of my contacts know I was holed up in a hospital in Mumbai. She reached me by phone a couple of days ago to let me know she'd been able to book a train from Pushkar to Mumbai and that she'd arrive in two days' time. It's actually great timing. Her travels have left her feeling a bit desultory. She needs a sense of purpose. She doesn't feel moved to begin volunteering, however, which is something we planned to do together. She is also ready to be around someone who knows her. She is in need of a friend, and I am in massive need of her love and support. I am also in need, desperate need, of the Percocet she is traveling with. She has been through two knee surgeries recently as a result of old soccer injuries, so she's traveling with Percocet. The doctors at Breach Candy Hospital won't give me anything stronger than ibuprofen for pain even though I am not sleeping due to the intensity of it. I've hardly slept since I've been here.

After the nurses clean up, the doctors make their rounds. If I am an outlier to Dr. Udwadia, then Ashley is four standard deviations from the mean. When he arrives to assess me with his coterie in tow, Ashley gives him the third degree.

"Why aren't you giving her anything for pain?" she demands, hands on her hips and ready to take him on.

Dr. Udwadia is clearly not used to a young female speaking to him in such a way (especially one with a tight T-shirt that reads SUB KUCH MILEGA, anything is possible). He gives her a once-over, left eyebrow slightly raised.

"We are giving her an anti-inflammatory. It's the inflammation that is causing the pain."

"She's in excruciating pain and has hardly slept since she's been here. It's not working," Ashley insists.

"We aren't giving her narcotics because they have side effects that are harmful."

"Harmful?" she challenges him, rolling her eyes.

I sink slowly into my covers, not sure I want to witness this.

"Patients become constipated and then they become nauseous, which means they won't eat. Their bowels slow down and this puts them at risk for developing a bowel obstruction. The outcome of this is worse than the pain. Furthermore, we need to treat the inflammation, not simply the pain. The inflammation is the cause of the pain. We will increase the anti-inflammatory that she is getting."

Back home we give narcotics out like they are candy because people in the West don't want to feel pain. It isn't really a part of our lives. We simply don't do discomfort well as a culture. Our culture doesn't know what to do with it because in general we haven't learned the proper tools that enable us to be with it differently. We don't believe we have the time, much less the capacity, for it. And sure, occasionally a patient becomes constipated, but then we treat that. Ashley doesn't press further. It's a moot point with the bottle of Percocet that's in her bag.

Once Dr. Udwadia leaves, we settle in with our mid-morning tea to catch up, to talk story. Ashley is able to make me laugh with the outlandishness of her adventures. I study her, taking in her appearance as she speaks to me. It seems that she has begun to transmute into something other than the young American I last saw in Boulder, Colorado. India has impacted her being. And her blue eyes sparkle with it. Traditionally, an Indian woman her age wouldn't be walking around in a shirt that tight. Otherwise her pants, her bracelets, her *bindi,* and her musical anklets seem to suggest that she is morphing. She seems more comfortable than I have ever seen her before.

So that you are familiar with dear Ashley, I'm going to give you some background. Picture this: Ashley at the age of seventeen, pinned under her car that she'd attempted to manually push by herself, in neutral, up the steep incline of her dirt driveway in the foothills just outside of Boulder. She'd decided to make a "test run," to see if she could get her car out of the driveway in preparation for sneaking out of the house at night without waking her parents. Her dad happened to be head of the Drug Task Force with the Boulder Police Department when this took place.

The car began to roll backward down the driveway, and somehow she fell as she tried to keep it from crashing into the house, pushing against the approaching car with all of her might. She was push-rolled down the hill with it. Eventually the car ran into the house, one of her hips pinned under it. She managed to walk away from this one with a mere broken pelvis.

Or picture Ashley at her seventh Burning Man in leather chaps. Or the time she was driving a Moped in traffic in Nepal and a bus began backing into her. She couldn't go anywhere because there was traffic behind her. Eventually when the bus stopped, its rear bumper was resting on her thigh as she tried desperately to brace herself against hitting the ground and having the Moped on top of her. Ashley's guardian angel has earned double overtime.

The underlying stress that comes from being sick and alone in India is insidious. With Ashley here, there is a degree of lightness that returns to my being. Mr. Gaikwad places a cot for Ashley at the foot of my bed against the wall. She unpacks her things, moving in like a roommate. She goes out late afternoon to run an errand and returns with a brilliantly colored bouquet of tropical flowers.

We discover a little worm that has made his edible home on the face of a large red flower. Something about that little guy trying to survive moves me. I feel a connection with him, trying to make it on his own in this big ole world. "Let's call him Pintoo," I say. This name comes from a worm I saw in a television commercial that Dan and I watched in one of the hotels where we were hiding out as refugees during one of my bouts of dysentery. Pintoo remains with us for the rest of our hospital stay. Every few hours we monitor his progress as he eats his little heart out. Day by day he grows bigger. I cheer him on.

"Yes, little guy," I say, "yes."

When Ashley stayed in a guesthouse in Pushkar in northern India, she arose early to do yoga each morning. Each day in the morning quietude she encountered a worker who was out doing a yantra. This worker chanted, "Yes, yes, yes, yes, yes, yes, yes ..." while pulling marigold petals from the flower and placing them in designs that spelled the word *yes*. I take that word on as my own yantra. It reminds me to allow. To let go and allow life to unfold without trying to restrict it, manipulate it, control it, or even to understand it. I need this whisper of wisdom to reach my heart with its subtle breath.

I receive two IV antibiotics in the evening. The first one is started at eight o'clock. The nightshift nurse comes in and takes my vital signs, hanging the antibiotic.

"I will be back in an hour to start the second one," she informs us.

No sooner is she out the door than Ashley and I are on our way outside. Ashley helps me into a standing position. She takes the IV pole in one hand and grabs a chair for me with the other. I follow behind her with my walker. Slowly we make our way outside through the glass doors onto the balcony. Until now, I'd only been able to gaze through these doors at the parrots, the seabirds, the merging water and sky.

Ashley places the chair so I can face the sea. I sit down cautiously. I feel the warm humidity of the Mumbai night on my skin as I breathe a sigh of relief to be seated outside. I hear the traffic, the honking horns. I can make out the sound of water moving in the darkness beyond. I am struck by life. It waits for no one. *Make haste slowly,* the wise ones say. Ashley pulls out her cigarettes. Sure, it'd be far better if I wasn't out here about to smoke a cigarette, but desperate times *do* call for desperate measures. We have managed to justify the outing to ourselves by calling it a "Smoke Ceremony." Native Americans do it as a form of cleansing and thanksgiving.

"First, let's declare our intentions." I begin. I inhale deeply, with eyes closed. Then I exhale into the night. "I would like to let go of fear and anxiety."

"May we let go of the negative mind," Ashley continues.

"I invite in love, compassion, and goodwill."

"I invite power and healing," says Ashley.

"May we know triumph," I say.

With our intentions declared, we each light up. We are the only people on the balcony. The night is an invitation into dark spaces made navigable by light.

"As we inhale, we inhale light," I say. "As we exhale, we exhale darkness."

We give thanks for our lives, for our friendship. We contemplate why we think this situation might have befallen me. And we don't pretend to know the half of it.

What I do know is that in reference to the adage "Ask and thou shall receive," the eternal *is* listening. So be careful what you ask for. Be darn sure you are ready to receive it. Because what you receive doesn't always look like you thought it might.

Since my early twenties, I've been asking the divine to help me evolve, to help me become more compassionate, kinder, more tolerant, less judgmental, to soften the edges, and not to add to suffering—mine or anyone else's. I remember lighting candles when I was in college in my quiet moments before bed. It was my version of meditation before I knew how to meditate. I would put forth my intentions with a one-pointed determination. I was hoping these things would just happen. Spontaneously happen. You know, flip of a light switch and poof. For me the journey apparently needs to be a little more difficult than that. Aries is Aries, and certain behaviors, certain ways of *being,* weren't going away on their own with my red fire energy. Leave it to a life-altering health opportunity to shake it up a little further, to bring me to my knees—no pun intended—and have me screaming *MERRRRCCCCY!* at the top of my lungs.

If we're open to it, we can unearth far deeper levels of understanding and clarity about ourselves and the fragile and mysterious thing we call life. Out of those depths of despair, those painful sharp edges that carve our canyons deep, arises a wellspring of wisdom. Structure loses structure. Form loses form. Lines are blurred into no lines. And reality is no longer three dimensional and linear. If we truly surrender to life, allow each moment to arise and pass away no matter what we're feeling—without assigning meaning or fixed belief, without needing to figure out, understand, or control— we hold the key to the secret of deep peace and happiness and all that underlies it. The key is in the allowing. The being with. The surrendering to.

I *thought* I'd surrendered during my first Vipassana course. What I now know is that there is a deepening, a quickening that happens gradually. We may learn something, but we continue to learn it over and over until we really get it. Until we've experienced it enough to truly figure it out for ourselves. Like getting sanded down softer and softer until there is nothing more to sand. If we turn our back on life's lessons, they keep showing up. The layers of the onion peel slowly and there are so many layers—

an unfathomable number of layers. It is essential to walk with heart open in order to experience all of it.

19

I finally graduate from a walker to crutches. I'm sleeping a little more each night thanks to Ashley's stash of Percocet. The dysentery has abated. After more than a week of sponge baths, I am ready to take my first shower. Ardi is slightly hesitant when I insist that I am able to make my way into a shower just down the hall, but Ashley and I are a tour de force, and Ardi is unable to say no.

There are several individual bathrooms with showers. Ashley takes my toiletries, a towel, and a clean pair of pajamas into one of the showers. I follow her down the hall slowly, smiling from my new sense of freedom and at being able to move around without a walker. With the motivation that the thought of a warm shower brings, I am able to put one foot in front of the other and make my way down the hall. My knees are stiff and painful. My feet don't seem to have the get-up-and-go they once did yet my determination is unwavering.

Ashley even went out and bought me new shampoo for the occasion. It is an Indian shampoo that smells like fragrant herbs and incense. I receive big smiles and nods of approval from the nurses and the "boys," all of whom are used to seeing me in more of a horizontal position. Mother Teresa peeks out from a room down the hall. The encouraging smile on her round face is so full of love. The bathroom is spacious and has a surprisingly clean tile floor and shiny white bathtub shower. There is a large frosted glass window through which beams the morning sunlight. The light gives the bathroom a fresh, airy feeling. A white plastic chair sits in the large bathtub.

"Ashley, will you make sure I get into that chair? I think I'll be okay after that."

"Sure thing," she replies, placing my shampoo and conditioner within reach.

I did not play team sports in high school so I didn't develop the indifference required to strip down and parade around the locker room without a hint of self-consciousness. I am one of those women who would rather change behind the safety of a bathroom stall. Here I am now, holding onto the wall and my crutches, stripping down in front of Ashley who isn't fazed at all.

No holds barred. I crutch over to the shower with my naked body. It requires two hands to lift each knee into a bend in order to clear the bathtub. Ashley already has the water running and with two hands I reach back for the plastic chair after she has taken my crutches. Slowly I lower my body into it. Terribly sharp pain sears through my knees as they are coerced into a ninety-degree angle. I begin the short little sequence of breaths that you see women performing in labor. The only thing I am birthing here, however, is a higher pain tolerance. Well, that and a new way of being.

"You okay?" she inquires.

I give her a thumbs-up. "Will you come back in about fifteen minutes?" I ask, as I manage to stretch my legs out before me.

"Yep," she says, and with that she pulls the curtain and leaves me sitting in the plastic chair under a warm stream of water.

I gaze at myself, at my physical body that has carried me faithfully through this life for thirty-two years. As the warm water drips off of my skin in the bright, soft morning light, I examine my breasts, my curvy hips, my swollen knees, and my thighs and calves that have already begun to atrophy. It feels like a lifetime has passed since I last showered on the tile floor of that hotel bathroom a week ago.

I inspect my physical body and for perhaps the first time in thirty-two years, I feel immense gratitude for it. I feel sadness for how hard I've been on myself so much of the time. I wrap my arms around myself and begin to cry. I rock back and forth in the warm water, hugging myself and telling myself how much I love me.

When I was a teenager I was embarrassed by the size of my boobs. I actually believed that perhaps a man would never love me because my boobs were small. And I grew up in a house where diet pills were kept in a drawer in the kitchen. I recall hearing from various members of my mom's side of the family, "Once on your *li-ips*, forever on your *hi-ips*," the lips and hips part sung out over two crescendo-decrescendo syllables for emphasis. As if eating a piece of cake or chocolate might condemn you for the rest of your life. I'd rather exude happiness and eat cake than spend my precious life energy obsessing about my weight, trying on at least seven different outfits before I leave the house because the one I really want to wear makes me look fat.

I recall being in an outdoor shower with one of my younger cousins when I was approximately eleven years old. I went through a chunky spell for a couple of years when I was that age. We stripped our bathing suits off to wash away the sand and the day at the beach. She looked at me and said, "Wow, your hips really *have* gotten big," no doubt echoing a conversation she must have overheard from the adults. No wonder I've had a body image issue my entire life, even though for most of it I've been what most people would consider fairly thin. I have *always* felt like I needed to lose weight. And that sense of "not being quite thin enough" is an insidious kind of dissatisfaction that eats away at your life force, your vital energy.

So here I am now, finally feeling love for my physical body just as it is—small boobs, curvy hips, and atrophied leg muscles. I thank it for faithfully carrying me through this life like a chariot, and I mean it. I promise myself, I actually *swear* to myself, there in that bathroom, that I am going to *love my body*. My temple. I also promise myself that the next time I walk around in a bathing suit I am going to do so with a confidence that I've only ever known when I graduated from high school at the age of eighteen weighing in at 118 pounds, way too thin for my five foot seven frame.

~

Ashley is traveling with her angel cards. You can pick from the deck of angel cards whenever the spirit moves you. You can think of it as something that the all-that-is is attempting to communicate to you. We made a practice of picking a card every morning together, usually during tea. After my shower, I am moved to pick an angel card. I pick SURRENDER.

Surrender is a practice. I might surrender in one moment only to resist in the next. And then I surrender to my resistance and unwillingness to surrender. Every time I encounter a moment with awareness and do indeed surrender to it, I am one step further along an eternally long path. "Willingly accept that which life presents." That was one of Dan's and my vows on our wedding day. It was a declaration of why we were choosing one another. It's not that we do this seamlessly in every situation all the time, but we keep returning to the opportunity to willingly accept that which life presents. We keep practicing. Keep returning. "Practice is perfect. Practice doesn't make perfect," says Lama Surya Das. To successfully surrender, you have to *want* to surrender. It is one of the hardest things to do. It sounds a hell of a lot easier than it is, but it does get easier with practice.

The shower is my first real activity in days. It was necessary for me to get moving at some point, but it was a little much—at least a little much for someone *not* taking narcotics for pain. I'm using Ashley's stash at night to help me sleep but not taking them during the day. I don't want to knock myself out. Since all I'm receiving from the nurses is the equivalent of ibuprofen, the pain I experience a few hours after the shower pushes the envelope of my tolerance. I move into complete aversion without remembering I'd ever heard the word *surrender*. *Fuck* begins to fly around liberally. The deflation that I thought I'd washed away with my shower rears its ugly head. I have to pee, but I can't imagine having to get out of bed again, so I hold it for hours. Try as I may I am unable to get a grip.

"*Please* take a Percocet," Ashley pleads. My somber attitude is wearing on her.

Finally I agree to take one, and Ashley heads out for a walk. At some point I fall asleep. I'm awakened by Ashley when she returns from her jaunt into the city. She is bearing mangos and flowers. The onslaught of phone calls begins. My mom, my brother, my father. Ashley watches me, phone call after phone call, going through all of the excruciating details with each person over and over again, each time growing more emotionally exhausted.

"You can't do this anymore," she declares. "It is wearing you out to have to go through all of the details with each member of your family."

She studies me for a moment.

"You need to decide who the point person is going to be, and that is who you are going to speak to. No one else. It's too wearing on you."

"Thank you, Ashley," I say with gratitude. Life gets a little easier.

~

Ashley and I are settled in having tea late that afternoon. She helped me get out of bed and into a big, comfortable, plastic reclining chair nestled in a corner of my room by the glass balcony door. The chair backs to the glass doors to the balcony, and my feet are propped up on the bed. Ashley has assumed a reclining position on the bed. We are chatting away when I follow Ashley's gaze over my shoulder and out the balcony door behind me.

There, gathered at the door with their faces pressed into the glass and peering in at us, are several Muslim women we recognize from a couple of days earlier. At that time, Ashley literally had to close the door on them as they tried to advance their way into my hospital room from the main corridor. Now they are trying a different approach—the balcony door. Clearly their curiosity has not been deterred by our Western standoffishness.

Initially I feel slightly annoyed. *Is it so difficult to give someone privacy?* Then the word *surrender* comes floating into my consciousness. I find myself softening. The irritation that besieged me seconds before loosens its vise as I turn and reach for the latch on the door. I open it and Ashley and I are face-to-face with the Muslim women wrapped in their *burkas*. Only one of them has her face bare; the others are behind cloth. The one with the bare face does all the talking.

"Are you the patient?" she asks in her thick Indian accent. She is studying me and my exposed arms and feet in my hospital pajamas. Her gaze moves from me to Ashley and back again.

"I am," I say.

"What has happened to you?" she inquires.

"I am having trouble walking," I answer, without going into too much detail.

"Where have you come from?" she asks.

"We are from the United States," I reply.

"My father is next door," she elaborates. "He has cancer in stomach."

Not a good diagnosis. I wonder if they are aware of this.

"Will you pray for him?" she asks.

"Yes, we will pray for him," I tell her, glancing at Ashley who is nodding in agreement.

"We will pray for you," she tells me.

When they are satiated with their knowledge of who we are and what we are doing in the room next door, they prepare to leave. I bow my hands in front of my face to them in a Namaste gesture, a common Indian greeting. I am quickly corrected.

"In our religion we say 'Insha Allah.'" She touches her fingers to her heart and her forehead.

Of course, I think to myself, *of course.* God willing. *Insha Allah.* And with that they turn and leave.

Allow. Surrender. Boundaries. No boundaries. We've all arisen from the same stuff—the same stuff to which we'll eventually return. The same stuff we already are. Our skin is merely an illusion of separation.

20

Ilie awake listening to Ashley's breath as she sleeps. Nighttime is surprisingly quiet here at Breach Candy. Most nights I can hardly detect any noise from the corridor.

I hear him just before he enters the room. I look toward the door and in the dark I watch it open. The tears begin. They are big, silent crocodile tears filled with a longing and a love so great that they burn as they leave my eyes. I know he is besieged by exhaustion, having boarded a plane less than twenty-four hours after arriving home from India. He flew around the world and returned to Mumbai at one o'clock in the morning.

Without saying anything, Dan pulls back the covers and makes his way into the hospital bed next to me. He nuzzles his face into my neck and holds me, his warm body pressed against mine. All I can do is cry. And all he can do is hold me. Eventually his embrace relaxes and his breath grows heavy, deep, and rhythmical.

When the sky turns gray I am still awake, Dan's arms around me. Ashley and Dan's breaths are a synchronized chorus. I gaze out at the ocean, just becoming visible. I *feel* India. The place that she is.

By the time Mr. Gaikwad comes with tea at six thirty, Ashley has awakened. We wake Dan and after he and Ashley have said their hellos, he moves to the cot and resumes his deep slumber. He doesn't budge for hours. He sleeps through breakfast, through the doctors' rounds, through my morning shower. He finally begins to move around lunchtime.

I am very self-conscious for the first few hours that we are together. When he left me, I was his able-bodied bride, about to take off by myself on a tour of India. Now I am a woman who cannot walk by herself, knees so swollen they cannot hold her own weight. I am sick and at times riddled with fear, anxiety, and tears.

He stands by as I fumble my way to the bedside commode. I am conscious of his eyes on me. I wonder what he is thinking, what he is feeling. There is no doubt in my heart that I've married the right man, but I feel insecure about being damaged goods that he'll want to return. I am not the woman with whom he ascended over twelve thousand feet from Boulder to Grand Lake on our bikes the summer before.

Over the past two days Ashley has gone searching for a guest-house for herself for a couple of nights because the hospital room is not big enough for the three of us. She has also started the search for a hotel for all of us when I discharge from the hospital. We need a room big enough for all of us to sleep comfortably. We need a decent toilet. We need a bathtub. And we need to be near the hospital so that I can take a taxi to and from outpatient physical therapy. This proves to be no small task. Mumbai is *the* most expensive city in India. Its hotel prices rival those of New York City. During the holiday season there is a high volume of weddings and the prices soar higher as availability dwindles.

It's good timing for Dan to be here because Ashley needs some time out. India is tiring by herself. Throw in the hunt for a quality hotel room during peak season and a sick friend who has required round-the-clock nursing care and psychological support. I'd need a break, too. She alone was charged with my well-being for days. She broke down in an Internet café yesterday, bawling to her mother over Skype.

After a good cry, she walked into a bakery, slightly exasperated after searching long and hard for hours for a place for us to call home. The bakery is the only clean remotely Western-appearing establishment she has seen. Its cakes, cookies, croissants, and quiche look like they could have been baked in France.

Enter Danesh and Perssus, the owners of the bakery. They also own the building that houses it. They are a couple in their mid-forties who are very successful entrepreneurs. After listening to our saga, they give Ashley samples of their baked goods to bring back to the hospital. And they send her to the Shalimar Hotel. The Shalimar is a half-mile from the hospital and has a two-room suite for us. It has a bedroom with an attached bathroom and a living area where Ashley can sleep.

"Come back when you are discharged from the hospital," Danesh and Perssus tell Ashley, "and we will lend you our DVD player and some movies"

Thank you, universe.

21

Finally the day of discharge is upon us. Dr. Jain's opinion is that I need to spend another week in India to grow strong enough to get on a plane and fly home. I am to follow up with him the day before we fly out. Dr. Udwadia and his entourage arrive to look me over one last time. I am sitting in the chair with my feet propped on the bed, and Ashley has reclined on the bed. Dan is down the hall taking a shower. The conversation turns to my thyroid level, which Dr. Udwadia wants to check because he thinks I am a little hyper.

"Dr. Jain tells me it is normal," I say.

"I believe you have been hyper since birth," Dr. Udwadia informs me.

I'm not hyper, I just have a lot of energy," I state, while he gazes at me with disbelief. "I'm going to write about this one day. I will send you a copy of my book when it's finished."

"What is this book about?"

"It is about my experience in India and the deeper meaning behind it."

"What meaning is this?"

"The spiritual meaning."

"You cannot come to India for one month and expect to gain spirituality, child. That takes time under great masters."

"I did not come to India seeking spirituality. I came to India because I felt moved to come here. I don't need to look outside of myself for anything."

"What is it you think about spirituality? God?" he asks me.

I was uncomfortable with the question because of the audience of young interns. I work within the world of Western medicine where one is often treated as a body part or ailment and not a human being experiencing a difficult, life-altering situation. Something big moved inside me and tears began to fall.

"I believe that there is one truth, that this truth is the divine. Different cultures call it different names and have decided upon different avenues to it. There are many paths to the top of the mountain," I say. I pause, catching my breath. "We're not separate from the divine, from God," I continue. "We arise from it. We *are* it. And that eternal truth is the present moment—the now—in all its forms of expression. Somewhere along the line humans began to perceive that we are separate from the divine. I think the root of the problem on our planet today is this sense of separation from the divine and the fear that results from it. People tend to be driven by that fear. It takes practice and discipline to reach a place where we feel this presence, this eternal now."

"Ahhh, that is a universal truth spoken by many," Dr. Udwadia says.

One of his interns becomes rather excited. "There is a theory about that called Advaita Vad," the intern states excitedly.

"Whose is it?" I ask.

"Adi Sankaracharya," he replies.

Adi Sankaracharya, I would later learn, lived from A.D. 788 to A.D. 820. His philosophy, called Advaita Vad, points toward a nondualistic ultimate reality—oneness. He certainly wasn't the first or the last to experience this reality. Many have experienced the oneness of things. Some live that reality, and some catch it in fleeting glimpses.

We aren't separate from the divine, or from each other for that matter. And we certainly don't need an intermediary to know this truth. We are all capable of knowing that which we already are, and of experiencing this divinity within ourselves. There is none among us who is more equipped to do the job. It's simply a matter of whether one is willing to do the work, to give enough space and silence to the heart to realize this truth experientially. When we experience it, we realize that mental labeling, projecting, fixed beliefs, old mental habit patterns, and sectarianism are actually hindrances to being that reality. If the medicine cures the illness, it does not matter where it comes from, the wise ones tell us.

There is a story passed down by Zen Master Seung Sahn who died in 2004. He says that when the mind is quiet, one connects with God. There is a meditation master, the story goes, who encounters a student after a meditation.

The student says to him, "I've been coming to this group for almost three years and I never connect with God. What is happening?"

The master replies, "Maybe your practice is not correct."

The student says, "No, no, my practice is correct. When *you* meditate, do you meet God?"

"Yes, yes, I meet God," says the master.

"Next time you meet God during your meditation, will you ask about me?"

"Yes," says the master. "I will ask God about you."

Next time after meditation this student appears.

"Master, Master, did you meet God?" he asks, excitedly.

"Yes, yes. I met God," replies the master.

"Did you ask God about me?" the student asks with great concern.

"I asked God about you. God said that your line is very busy."

If you want to connect with God, says Zen Master Seung Sahn, put down your line.

~~~

The excited young intern was still going on about Advaita Vad, when Dr. Udwadia interrupted him to lecture me.

"Remember, child, when you are well again … *slowly, slowly.* And tell your President George W. Bush what you just told me."

"I didn't vote for him."

"Let me see how you are doing," he says with a warm smile. He listens to my chest and feels the glands in my neck. He looks at my knees one last time.

"How do you feel?" he asks.

I decide to show him. I grab my crutches that are leaning against the glass door behind me. I make my way to a standing position. Once I am standing I turn to look at him. I realize with surprise that I am looking down on him by a couple of inches. He seemed so tall, so big in character to me all of this time.

"Good, good," he says.

Dr. Udwadia turns to leave, followed by his interns. He turns around before he walks out of the room and asks, "Do you know what the difference is between the Americans and the British?"

"No, I don't. What is the difference between the Americans and the British, Dr. Udwadia?"

"The British are so very formal," he states, as he eyes Ashley lounging on the bed and me back in the chair with my legs propped up, baring the soles of my feet, which is considered quite unholy in Eastern religious traditions. There is a smile in his eyes.

Dan returns from his shower. He and Ashley pack my belongings in my backpack. As we await the arrival of our nurse to go over the discharge instructions, and the arrival of Mr. Gaikwad with the wheelchair to take me downstairs, I am seated on the bed facing my little glass door, gazing out at the Arabian Sea, which has been a harbinger of hope.

"Do you want to see it?" Dan asks me.

"I can't," I reply, thinking it would have been nice to see the common area at the end of the balcony where Ashley had gone every morning to do her yoga.

Dan approaches me. "Come on," he says, and with that he lifts me off of the bed and into his arms. He walks out onto the balcony and I feel like Debra Winger in *An Officer and a Gentleman* as my beautiful husband carries me down the length of the balcony, my arms wrapped around his neck, my long hair blowing in the breeze of the hot Mumbai afternoon. Patients and their family members crowd their doorways to the balcony to catch a glimpse of the Americans who are displaying behavior fit for a Hollywood love scene. As Dan is approaching the ledge, Ashley snaps a picture from behind. She catches a bird in flight. The image of that bird in flight becomes something I hold close in my heart.

Dan places me gently at the edge where I hold fast to the wall and search the deep blue mysterious expanse of water that has sustained me during my time in the hospital. It is midday and the water is filled with tiny whitecaps from the breeze. While I couldn't be happier to be leaving the hospital, there is nostalgia in my heart as I say goodbye to all of it. I'm aware that major changes in my life are upon me, and I feel reverence as I say goodbye to this place, to the people who cared for me in my darkest hour.

Then comes Mr. Gaikwad barreling down the balcony with the wheelchair screaming, "Sorry! Sorry! Sorry!" (sounding like Sawdee! Sawdee! Sawdee!) and does not stop apologizing until he has me sitting safely in his chair. Needless to say, I generously pad the pockets of my kind, dependable, ever-smiling friend upon our departure. God *is* great, Mr. Gaikwad. And so are you.

22

We settle in at the Hotel Shalimar. To celebrate emancipation from the hospital I decide I'd like to have lunch in the hotel restaurant.

"Maybe it'd be better if we just order room service," Ashley suggests gently. Dan nods in agreement.

"Maybe it would be, but I have been cooped up for too long. I'd like to try to make it down there," I reply. "It'll be my physical therapy for the day."

After a few minutes we are on our way down to the restaurant. It is slow going with the crutches, but I am determined to get there. I order *saag*—my favorite Indian dish, while Dan and Ashley each order a fair amount of food as well. We eat like kings, Dan trying India's version of Chinese food, since he is still not eating the mush. The conversation eventually turns to marriage.

"It's true what they say about marriage, Ashley," Dan says. "You get married and you really *do* stop having sex."

Laughing, I nod in agreement as I ponder this. As soon as we were married in September I developed a low back injury from nursing that resulted in Dan having to carry my backpack during our honeymoon, and in turn I carried his tiny daypack. Then we get to India and each of us has our turn with dysentery. Now four months into our marriage my knees are in such bad shape I couldn't make love to my husband even if I wanted to.

After our meal, we're exhausted. We plug in the DVD player that Danesh and Perssus lent us and settle in to watch a movie. It is difficult for me to get comfortable in any position, so I finally lower myself to the floor from the couch. When the movie ends and it is time for bed, I physically cannot get myself off the floor. My knees don't want to bend and they're swollen and excruciatingly painful.

I try to use the couch to hoist myself upright but am unable to do so because that would require bending my knees. I begin to cry, then sob. I'm experiencing more exhaustion, pain, and frustration than I have the capacity to handle at the moment. Dan approaches me to try to help and I forcefully push him away. I'm ashamed. Ashamed that I am unable to function like a normal person, ashamed that I have to be picked up off of the floor.

For better or for worse, in sickness and in health, I think to myself, wishing it were as easy as it sounds. Eventually Ashley kneels down by my side. She cups my face in her hands and says, "You have to let us help you." She says it with compassion but also with an air of authority. She is the nurse. I am the patient. Dan and Ashley each take a side and hoist me, dead weight, from the ground to a standing position.

When in the throes of an acute inflammatory process, a little bit of activity goes a long way. The following morning my knees are in such bad shape that I am unable to go to physical therapy at the hospital. That would necessitate getting to the lobby and into a cab, and I do not have it in me. It's just as well because I'm feeling up to a pity party. There are no invites going out either. Dan and Ashley are going to walk around the city a little, and I'm looking forward to the time alone. I'm in a funk and have no intention of getting out of it anytime soon. I'm ready to do some serious sulking.

Before Dan and Ashley leave, they help me get set up at the table by the window in our makeshift living room that doubles as Ashley's bedroom. I am quite pleased with my cache of water, Coke, cigarettes, journal, and space from other human beings. The floor-to-ceiling window has no screen and I slide it wide open. The warmth of the Mumbai sun filters through. I begin chain-smoking and bird watching. There seem to be endless birds soaring around the sky, possibly more birds in the sky over Mumbai than I have seen anywhere in my life. It could be because Mumbai is built on a series of seven merged islands or because the Parsees in India place their dead on top of a building here, called the Tower of Silence, to be eaten by vultures.

Within the ancient Zoroastrian tradition, a dead body is considered a filthy thing. Zoroastrians believe that a corpse demon enters it and pollutes anything the body might come into contact with. By placing the dead body on top of a Tower of Silence, the sun and the birds are able to dispose of the body before the process of decomposition can happen, thereby preventing pollution of the earth. It is comforting watching those birds soar around through the warm currents above me, regardless of whether they are actually guarding me from contamination by a dead person's corpse demon. I spy two green parrots on a wire just down the street.

My real source of entertainment becomes an eleven-story apartment building across the street from the hotel. I am able to voyeur myself into everyday life. I watch an old man in his kitchen in a white undershirt preparing food for his family. Young men lean against the outdoor stairwell smoking cigarettes and talking on cell phones. They watch me watch them. When a few of them gather to sit and smoke and simply observe me, I grow uncomfortable and pull the curtain in front of me to obscure their view. That apartment building is better than daytime television.

Later that afternoon I make my way back to bed. I'm only able to sit up for so long in a chair before my knees get stuck at ninety degrees. And in the bed at least I can mow the grass with my knees and get a little physical therapy in. I think I've sufficiently worked through the pity party. Nothing a liter of Coke and a pack of Gold Flake cigarettes can't fix. That and the birds, of course. Sitting by that window observing life unfold as those birds soar around endlessly makes all this bearable. Besides, a pity party can be a lonely place. Dan refuses to join me there. It's a rule of his.

I am hanging out in bed when Dan and Ashley arrive home from their adventure. Ashley spent most of the morning in an Internet café while Dan roamed around the city. While trying to navigate his way out of a throng of people by winding his way off of the main drag into the backstreets, he wound up in a slum surrounded by a sea of young men in white. "Little big men," he says of them, referring to the fact that they were barely adolescent and had the maturity and articulation of well-educated men. Apparently, they were having a festival to celebrate their coming-of-age, and as part of that they give back to the community. So they grabbed Dan's hand and wound him around their temple, their booths set up with water for those less fortunate. They handed Dan a cup of "holy" water and said, "Drink!" And he drank.

"It *looked* clean," he says.

I am listening to this tale of adventure when I break out into a cold sweat and am forced upright by an all-too-familiar sensation. A crampy, achy, gastrointestinal urge that I have been wrought with far more times than is humane or acceptable in the last several weeks, spreads throughout my abdomen.

The bathroom is right at the end of the bed. But getting to the bathroom is no small feat, and I no longer have the luxury of a bedside commode. To get to the bathroom I first have to mow the grass, which can take at least a couple of minutes *per* leg. I am finally making my way to the edge of the bed when I glance at Dan and Ashley who are standing by, not sure quite what to do. Their expressions force me to turn around and see for myself. There is a brown trail following me from my pillow to the edge of the bed. Sometimes you are left with precious few options, and Ashley bursts into laughter. Then I burst into laughter. Dan is standing there with a concerned look on his face, not sure how to react. My laughter turns to tears.

I am forced to call Dr. Jain and begin antibiotic round three (ding-ding-ding). And then I am forced to ask my husband the unthinkable.

"Dan?"

"Yes, Molly?" he says in his most patient, loving voice.

"Will you do me a favor?"

"Yes, Molly," he replies, still sounding like the most patient and loving husband on the planet.

"Would you go down to the chemists and see if they have any adult diapers?"

He doesn't flinch. "Sure I will," he says, in a voice so calm that you might have thought I just asked him to run out for salt. He's become good friends with the chemist, maybe even customer of the year. The chemist is a couple of blocks away. It is where Dan has gone to get all of my various medications, where he buys the saltine-like biscuits that I keep next to the bed on the nightstand so that I can take my gut-havoc-wreaking anti-inflammatories first thing in the morning before breakfast. I figure it'd be better for me to sleep in diapers than have Dan and Ashley change the entire bed again. I imagine what the Indians washing my sheets must think. "Those Americans, they are *lazy* people," I imagine them bantering back and forth.

Dan returns from the chemist with the adult diapers. He helps me lift my hips to get the diaper on just so. I stare at his soft, determined face, at those deep, green eyes as he fastens the diaper in place. He looks at me and gives me a gentle smile. "We'll get through this," he says. I half believe him. Talk about surrender.

~⁓

Several days later Dr. Jain clears me to fly home. I visit him in his office at the hospital one last time, and I grow teary as I thank him for his excellent care. How blessed I am to have been under the treatment of one who cares so deeply about my well-being.

"You *will* walk without your crutches," he assures me. "And you must remember to smile."

The day of my departure Ashley and I have a sit-down, just the two of us. We smoke a couple of cigarettes for ole times' sake.

"You're a rock star, Ashley. Thanks for everything. I truly don't know what I would have done without you."

"*You're* the rock star, Molly. Don't forget it. And when you get home—*slowly, slowly.*"

She returns to her journey, alone, at the age of twenty-six. She travels south to Kerala in southwest India to a yoga Ashram. Eventually she'll head back to Rishikesh in northern India where she'll meet an Indian man. He'll be the man she'll marry, the man whose child will be growing inside of her when she arrives back in the U.S.

Dan and I leave the Shalimar Hotel in a taxi bound for the airport that night. We drive through the streets of Mumbai in the dark one last time. I know that I have to go home and recover from the illness, but I am not thrilled to be leaving India. She has become a friend. A teacher. She broke me—cracked the shell, so to speak. She stirred the pot, dredging up old, solid structures that want to crumble. She has afforded me the opportunity to remember how exquisitely precious each moment of this brief human life is, how precious the many blessings that we don't see most of the time. Because of her I can no longer ignore that my purpose on this planet has everything to do with what is going on inside. And there is a lot going on in there.

There is rainstorm and sun, and deep blue skies the hues of which my conscious mind has only dreamt of experiencing. There is rich, fertile soil juxtaposed with sand from a desert devoid of moisture. There is light so bright it is blinding, and darkness so complete it feels impenetrable. There is wild laughter from a heart untamed and free, and despair so deep that it brings me to my knees with the weight of its chains and suffering. There are birds singing revelry, and coyotes howling at the bright, full moon. There are frogs croaking their delight because they're submerged in mud up to their eyeballs, and sweet cats curled up in late afternoon sunshine streaming through a glass window. There are a million honking cars on a busy street in Mumbai, and if I pause—underlying all of it is a quiet stillness so vast that it teeters on the edge of extinguishing it all.

Ashley

Me, Dr. Vibha, Ashley

Dan, Danesh, Perssus, Ashley

Dan sweeping me off of my feet

Dan, Mr. Gaikwad, me

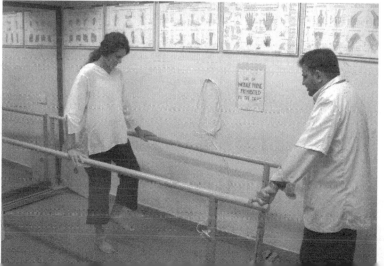

Learning how to walk in India with the help of Anish

2010

2015

Acknowledgments

Mom, thank you for your time, patience, and care watering my roots, and for providing space, guidance, and support for me to discover my wings. Words fail to express the depth of my love and gratitude.

My beloved Dan, thank you for teaching me about (and humbling me by) your display of the unconditional. For making room for all of me.

Jody Berman, thank you for polishing my manuscript with your incredibly talented editorial skills. Susan Wasinger, thank you for your gifted artistic and design skills— for taking my vision and turning it into a gorgeous cover and for the interior design of my book.

To all of the rest of my peeps— there are far too many to name here— thank you for your exquisite presence in my life and for helping my heart expand.

DISCLAIMER

There is a poem I love called "Desiderata" by the late Max Ehrmann. *"You are a child of the universe, no less than the trees and the stars,"* it says. Like us all, I am a child of life, of existence, of eternity—no less than the trees and the stars.

Vipassana meditation has been a tool for me, a sharp one at that. But that is what it is. I am not a Buddhist. I am not a "Vipassana meditator." I've been moved to sit these courses and I continue to benefit from so doing.

In this book, I refer to the proverbial "top of the mountain." In reality, there is no top of the mountain because there is nowhere to go. Nowhere to "get to."

Hands in front of my heart, in reverence and gratitude, I bow to you.

Made in the USA
Charleston, SC
23 February 2016